GOLF
IN SCOTLAND
IN THE BLACK & WHITE ERA
BY STEVE FINAN

ISBN 978-1-84535-900-3

First published in Great Britain in 2022 by DC Thomson & Co., Ltd., Meadowside, Dundee, DD1 9QJ.

Copyright © DC Thomson & Co., Limited.

All rights reserved. No part of this publication may be reproduced, stored in a retrieval system, or transmitted by any means, without the prior permission in writing of the copyright holder, nor be otherwise circulated in any form of binding or cover other than that in which it is published. This book is sold on the condition that it — and especially the photographs within it — will not, by way of trade or otherwise, be posted online, resold, hired out, lent or otherwise distributed, or circulated in any form or style. We are watching.

Main text Copyright © 2022 DC Thomson & Co., Ltd.

COVER/BACK COVER DESIGN | LEON STRACHAN

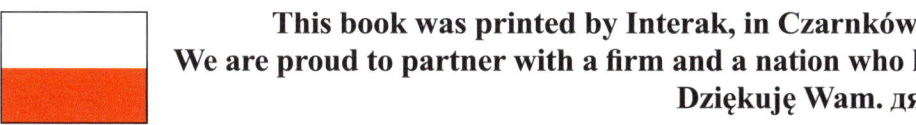

This book was printed by Interak, in Czarnków, Poland, in March and April, 2022. We are proud to partner with a firm and a nation who have done so much for Ukrainian refugees. Dziękuję Wam. дякую.

The DC Thomson copyright photographs in this book are available to buy from:

www.photoshopscotland.co.uk

Foreword by Colin Montgomerie, OBE

SINCE I turned professional in 1987, I have won over 50 times, been the European Tour No.1 eight times and won the Ryder Cup both as a player and as a captain.

But the one thing that has made all these achievements extra-special is being able to fly the flag for Scotland around the world.

I'm a proud Scotsman and I'm always happy to tell people about my country and what it gives to the world.

I was born here, I learned to play the game here and, despite now spending much of my time playing in the United States, I still come home regularly.

I love Scotland, and I love its golf courses.

But, very strongly, I also love our country's golfing history.

I don't profess to be any sort of "golf historian" by any means. I simply enjoy reading about it and looking back on the game as it used to be.

That's why I was so excited to get a sneak peek at this fantastic book.

On the following pages you'll find some incredible pictures that you won't have seen before, featuring some of the most famous names in the game – but all on golf courses you perhaps might not recognise at first glance.

It's a fascinating look at the game in all its glory, featuring never-before-seen photography from the best in the business.

It provides a wonderful, visual reference of what golf was like in "the good old days".

If you're anything like me, you'll find yourself taking a close look at all of the little details as they were back then, and comparing them to how things look today.

The Road Hole bunker at St Andrews, for example, and the buildings that line the famous 18th hole of the Old Course.

It is, in short, a wonderful, nostalgic walk down memory lane and a reminder that, though we all come and go, this great game has long endured and will continue to do so.

Now, put your feet up and enjoy!

Colin Montgomerie, 2022

■ Monty and Lee Trevino on St Andrews' 18th green during the 1990 Open.

Finding old golf photographs

THESE days, hundreds of thousands of digital photographs are taken whenever any player of note steps on to a course. This wasn't the case in the days of black and white photography.

Professional newspaper photographers were tolerated, although well warned to refrain from disturbing play.

Amateur snappers were frowned upon in case their cameras' whirring and clicking (heaven forfend there might be flash bulbs!) distracted the players.

These days, a digital sports photographer might offer their publication a choice of several thousands of photos from a major tournament.

In the 35mm era, four or five rolls of film might be shot. In the older days of gelatin dry plate negatives, a mere handful might have been taken.

So there is a limited supply of old golf photos. Those that do exist you will have seen again and again in newspapers, magazines, books and on websites.

A collection of "new" old photos, therefore, is a very rare thing. But that's what this is. Photos that have lain unlooked at for 40, 50, 60 years or more.

I am warned against using terms like "dusty" and "forgotten" when referring to shelves of photo packets, as these are insults to the skills and working practices of archivists. The archive at DC Thomson, where the majority of these photos were held, is a (professionally curated) Aladdin's Cave. And kept clean!

The photos might have been out of sight, but they weren't lost. The negatives were merely waiting for someone to come along to painstakingly examine them all with a lightbox and magnifying glass.

That someone was me. I have spent years in the DC Thomson archive. This book is the result.

■ **This is The Open at Muirfield in 1966.**

Not every photo in the archive was a good one, not every photo was interesting. I peered at negatives uncounted, seeking gems.

This is not a history book and was never intended to be. It is certainly not an account of every event in Scottish golf history.

It is a photo-led nostalgia book.

The intention is to show how golf looked in its home country in the old days. This is how older golfers remember it. The photos also show the game in a way younger golfers will never have experienced.

There has never been a Scottish golf book like this. Unless a time machine is invented, there never can be again.

Steve Finan, 2022.

Dedication

THIS book is dedicated to a group of people, without whom a book like this would not be possible: archivists.

Indeed, no book that deals with historical matters would be possible without recourse to the material held in archives.

Archivists are too rarely celebrated or properly thanked. They have encyclopaedic knowledge, incredible powers of recall, and (in my experience) a proactive approach that greatly improves every project we undertake together.

This book is, therefore, dedicated to David Powell, Barry Sullivan, Gary Thomas, Mollie Horne, Katie Thompson, Melissa Lonie, Kirsty Smith, and Irina Florian – the archives team at DC Thomson & Co. Ltd.

Thank you, friends.

■ **Golf on Kings Links, Aberdeen, in 1948.**

Further thanks to

Colin Montgomerie for a fantastic and insightful foreword.
Leon Strachan, artist extraordinaire.
My readers and sense-checkers Jock Gardiner, Ian McPherson, and Albert MacKenzie.
Neil Meldrum, for his impressive golfer-identifying expertise.
Kevin McQuillan.
Michael McEwan.
Bryce Ritchie.
Craig Houston.
Gill Martin.
Sylwia Jackowska.
Jacqui Hunter.
James Kirk.
Nikki Fleming.
Ryan Law.
Graeme McEwing.
Connor Vearnals.
Julie-Ann Marshall.
My personal thanks to Carole, Rebecca, and Lewis Finan.
David Finan.
Rod Finan.
John Jamieson.
Bill and Chris Nicoll.
David Nicoll.
Frank Chalmers.
Bob Seith.
David Patterson.
Fraser T. Ogilvie.

Steve Finan, 2022.

CONTENTS

THE OLD COURSE

THE WORLD'S OLDEST AND MOST FAMOUS GOLF VENUE

PAGE 12

THE 1950s

CHARISMA OF PETER THOMSON, BOBBY LOCKE AND BEN HOGAN

PAGE 80

BABE ZAHARIAS IN SCOTLAND

THE MOST NATURAL ATHLETE EVER TO WALK A FAIRWAY

PAGE 132

PRE-1950s

GREAT DAYS OF BOBBY JONES

PAGE 48

IRONS LADIES

HEROES OF THE WOMEN'S GAME

PAGE 114

ST ANDREWS

A GOLF TOWN WITH A QUITE INCREDIBLE HISTORY

PAGE 138

CARNASTY

LOCALS ARE PROUD OF THEIR FEARSOME GOLF COURSE

PAGE 170

THE 1960s

THE WONDERFUL YEARS OF 'THE BIG THREE'

PAGE 196

THE 1970s

THE SCOTTISH GAME CATCHES UP WITH THE USA

PAGE 246

ST ANDREWS FROM ABOVE

AERIAL SHOTS OF THE OLD COURSE THROUGH THE AGES

PAGE 278

THE CHANGING FACE OF THE GAME

FOR BETTER OR WORSE, GOLF ISN'T LIKE IT USED TO BE

PAGE 298

GOLF IS AN ALL-WEATHER SPORT

THE GAME CARRIES ON IN SCOTLAND, NO MATTER WHAT!

PAGE 334

12

The Old Course

THE 150th Open Championship, in July 2022, was played over The Old Course, St Andrews. The 30th time the course hosted the tournament. Where else could such an anniversary be marked but the home of golf, where the game has been played since the 15th Century?

Scotland takes pride in St Andrews. It is a jewel in the nation's crown (see page 138).

On a worldwide scale, however, the town is overshadowed by a thin strip of links land that doglegs out from a street named Golf Place, hooks around far out on the windswept peninsula towards the River Eden estuary, and doubles back on itself.

The Old Course, the Grand Old Lady – the first golf course in the world.

It isn't, at first, much to look at. When rolling into town by rail for the first time in 1946 (on his way to winning that year's Open) the great Sam Snead looked out of the carriage window and said: "Say, that looks like an old abandoned golf course!"

But golf isn't a beauty contest. It is a measure of skill, of resolve and, as they describe bravery in Scotland, a test of "bottle".

No other course has so many legends. No course has so many notable features – anyone who ever swung a club has heard of The Road Hole, The Seven Sisters, The Valley of Sin, Miss Grainger's Bosoms, The Spectacles, and The Elysian Fields.

No other course has a 700-year-old footbridge, the Swilcan Bridge – the most photographed golf course feature in the world.

Every other course on the planet has 18 holes because, from 1764, The Old Course has had 18 holes and that became the standard. Indeed, it is sometimes said that every other golf course in the world is merely a copy of The Old Course.

Very few sports have an identifiable, still-existing, still-accessible origin point and central focus in the way that golf has St Andrews. This is holy ground.

■ **Right: a plan of the Old Course produced for spectators at the 1953 Open.**

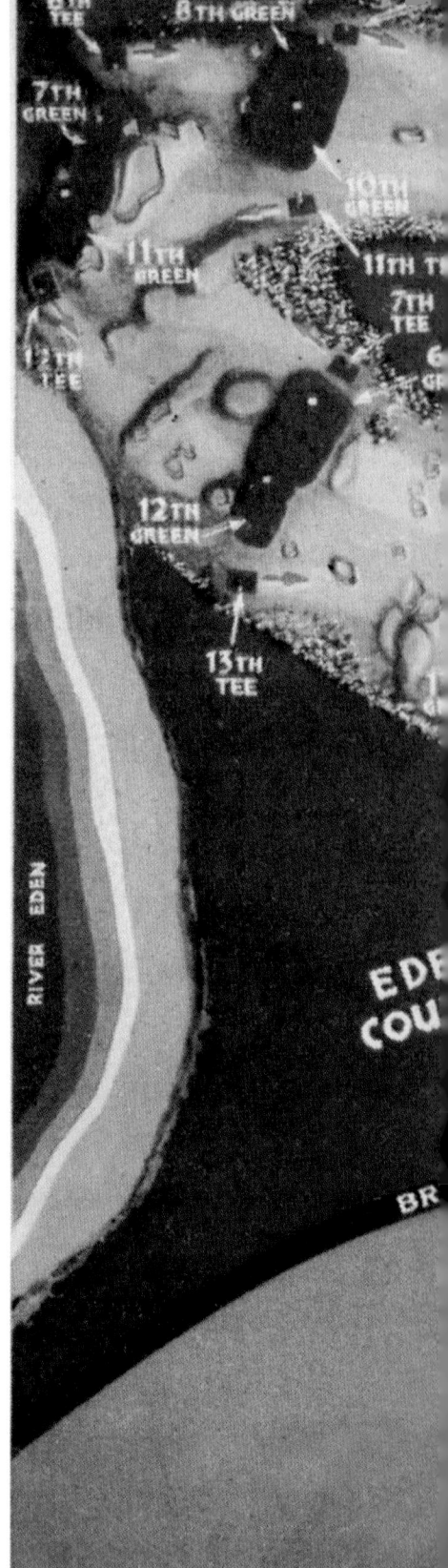

St Andrews Old Course

THE Royal & Ancient Clubhouse has appeared in millions of photos over the years. It is golf's most recognisable building.

Much ceremony was afforded to the laying of the foundation stone on July 13th, 1853.

Major John Whyte-Melville of Bennochy and Strathkinness, a venerable R&A member, led a procession through the town from Madras College. The townspeople turned out in numbers to watch.

Major Whyte-Melville was a member of the R&A for 67 years, from 1816 until his death at the age of 85, and quite a character. He was captain in 1823 and a full-length portrait of him hangs in the R&A.

The major was famous for playing two games a day, on two days of every week, and never – without exception – calling off a game for such a minor detail as adverse weather.

His son George (who would also be a captain of the club) went on to be a celebrated novelist in Victorian times. Few these days read his works, but his magnum opus *Digby Grand* was a best-seller in its time.

On the day of the foundation-laying, with great aplomb (and, clearly, a sense of theatre) Major John Whyte-Melville smote that first stone a ringing blow with a mallet and called for: "the Great Architect of the Universe to shower down his blessing upon this work".

Construction took 11 months from start to finish, with the club ready to open on June 22nd, 1854.

The Royal & Ancient promote and support the game in Scotland and around the world. They are also, having established the World Golf Museum, the guardians of the history of the game. The R&A is an institution that all golfers of all nations can be proud of.

■ **This photo of the clubhouse is from 1947.**

■ Peter Thomson putts out to win the 1955 Open, in the shadow of the R&A. Peter finished two strokes ahead of Scotland's Johnny Fallon.

The name of the tournament is just that – The Open. There is no need to add "British" or "UK". It was, for many years, the only major. Other open championships are identified by the name of their country to distinguish them from the original.

■ **These two pages (and the following two-page spread) are photos taken during the 1955 Open.**

It is an altogether more staid and quiet occasion compared to the global event The Open would become.

In those days, the championship took place on a Wednesday, Thursday and Friday, with two rounds (morning and afternoon) on the Friday.

The last three-day Open was 1965 (at Royal Birkdale).

The final round was switched to a Saturday the following year (Muirfield) and The Open fell into line with the other Majors in 1980 (again Muirfield), when play moved to the now-familiar Sunday finish.

■ **Another shot of the 1955 Open.**

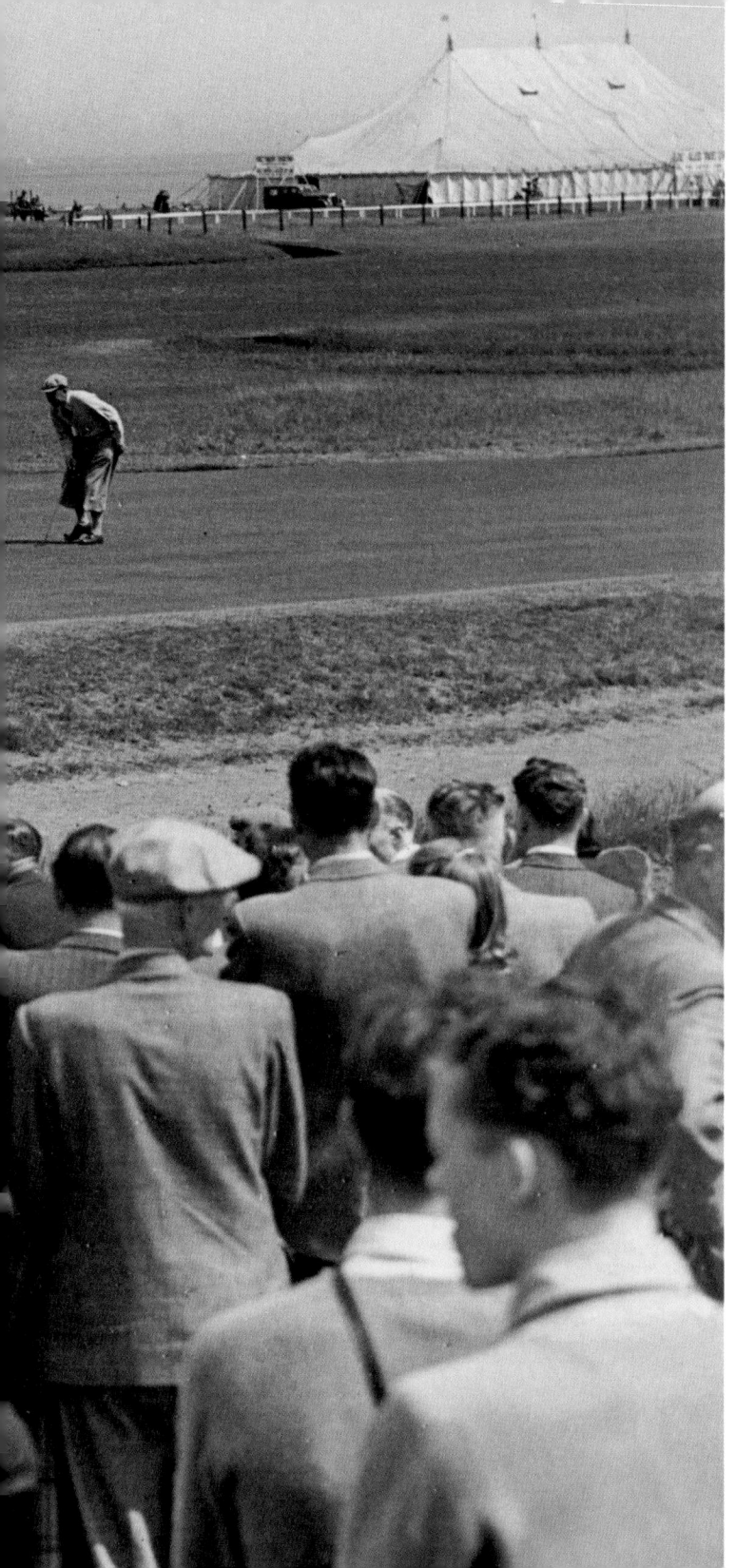

■ **This is the first post-war Open, in 1946.**

The gallery stands apparently quiet and respectful. But there were rumblings about crowd etiquette. Jack Harkness, the leading sports reporter in Scotland at the time, wrote:

When it was all over I held a post-mortem with starter Jimmy Alexander. "Don't blame Dai Rees," said Jimmy. "You can put his fatal start down to an ignorant spectator. Dai's driver was back and the downward swing had just started when a raucous voice shouted — 'Go to it, Welshman.' Dai then staged his only slice at the first tee in the whole tournament. Jimmy told me he went to look for this spectator, with the intention of having him put off the course. But Jimmy didn't get his man!

Rees let the incident pass without comment. But another spectator roused the ire of Australia's Norman von Nida. Disturbed while putting at the Road Hole, von Nida singled out the offender, and gave him a dressing down. Not content with that, he played out the last hole — and promptly returned to the seventeenth to settle the argument. He arrived just as Rees holed his putt for a birdie 4 in that record-breaking 67. Which provided an amusing angle, for, as I said, "Well done," an old lady standing at my side said, "Hush! Mr von Nida has just told us we mustn't talk!"

And while I'm on the subject of noises, here's a suggestion to the R. and A. As the last and very important green at St Andrews is so near the main road to the official car park, can't a "No Hooting of Horns" regulation be introduced? And, of course, there's a fortune awaiting the chap who can invent a noiseless camera — though those padded ones of the cine men come mighty near it.

■ **Left: South African Bobby Locke and Australian Joe Kirkwood Snr putting out on the 17th.**

■ The extent and depth of the Valley of Sin in front of the 18th green is sometimes difficult to see in photos. But with spectators standing around it, a better perspective is gained. This photo is from 1970.

■ **The Open of 1939.**

Over the years, newspapers and magazines have attempted to explain or give a wider understanding of holes and hazards with "graphics" pointing out the salient features of courses.

In pre-digital days, when photo manipulation wasn't easy, this was done by artists working on actual photographs – with varying levels of success.

This pre-war Old Course graphic is better than some, though a far cry from the modern examples you will see. It has a certain charm, though.

There are several more aerial views of the course in a chapter starting on page 278.

■ A less-often-seen view of the 1st fairway, taken from a point alongside the clubhouse in 1962.

THE demise of the course-side railway track in 1969 changed The Old Course's character a little.

The essence of golf course design is taking the natural lie of the land and moulding a course on to it, while also shaping the land to become a course. Each set of geographical features is different.

The same is true of surrounding, sometimes encroaching, features such as streams that cross the course, stands of trees, or nearby high ground that might affect the behaviour of the wind.

A railway track that is a danger for wayward shots gives a course – for good or ill – part of its personality. The noise of passing trains (some courses have to be played with huge jet aeroplanes landing close by) is also something that has to be taken into account.

So it follows that The Old Course when the railway was there (the track opened in 1852 and remained for 117 years) played differently to when it wasn't there.

This photo shows the 15th and 3rd green in 1955.

Image: GMC-11-19-4. Courtesy of the University of St Andrews Libraries and Museums

■ **Getting to the cut-and-thrust of playing the Old Course. This photo and the following three show close-up views of specific parts of the course as they were in 1947. This is the 16th and 2nd green. Then, as now, you might end up attempting the longest putt of your entire golf career on a St Andrews green.**

■ This is the 15th and 3rd green. It has evolved over the years (as all greens on all courses do) and is a little different – but still very recognisable – today. As any good caddy will advise, your tee-shot on the 15th should be aimed at the church spire.

■ 1947 again. The 7th and 11th green. Finding yourself in the position this golfer is in can be very tough – as many a great name has found out. Go long on the 11th and you are in deep trouble.

■ **The vast 13th and 5th green in 1947. The 13th, locals will tell you, is the most underestimated hole on the course. Be very careful here. The 5th, by contrast, should be easier . . . as long as you avoid the Seven Sisters.**

■ **As with all golf courses, The Old Course is repaired and bunkers rebuilt when needed.**

It is part of the greenkeepers' craft to decide when minor or major work requires to be done, and what (if any) changes to the character of the hazard are required.

This photo shows the Shell Bunker at the 7th, one of the four largest bunkers on the course, being re-turfed in 1935.

Almost all of the work was done manually in those days.

Image: GMC-11-11-6. Courtesy of the University of St Andrews Libraries and Museums

36

■ Hell Bunker on the 14th being re-banked in 1957. It perhaps looks even more formidable than it does now!

Image: GMC-11-23-3. Courtesy of the University of St Andrews Libraries and Museums

■ Two shots of the 17th in August 1967, just as the old railway sheds are being replaced by what was then termed "The Railway Hotel" that would become The Old Course Hotel. The best chance of an easier approach is a blind tee shot over the sheds. Stay left, and your second shot has to be incredibly accurate to carry the frightening 'Sands of Nakajima' pot bunker but hold without spilling on to the tarmac road.

■ The Old Course has had a huge influence on course design around the world. The philosophy of the 17th is probably the most copied aspect. The trade-off between the level of conservatism off the tee affecting the degree of difficulty in your second shot is mirrored at courses from Japan to Florida. They all took their inspiration from a stretch of grass, a couple of sheds, a roadway, and a few patches of sand in north-east Fife.

■ The picturesque Swilcan Bridge is so old, no one quite knows what it is properly called. It was built more than seven centuries ago and crosses what Ordnance Survey (the national mapping agency of Great Britain) lists as the Swilken Burn (note the different spelling). For hundreds of years it was called merely "The Golfer's Bridge" but you'll also find it named The Swilcanth in older reference books. It is routinely treated with respect, indeed reverence, by golfers from the very greatest downwards. It is an unusual player who, when crossing it for the first time, doesn't put a hand on the parapet to "feel" the history. It connects the two stretches of the 18th fairway, but also connects the game's earliest origins to what golf has become today.

■ 1978. Head greenkeeper Walter Woods stands in the notorious Hill Bunker by the 11th green. This was the bunker at which, during the 1921 Open, the great Bobby Jones (then aged 19 and a little known young American) ripped up his card after four attempts to play his way out. It was his first Open.

■ In 1972 the 10th was re-named in honour of a man who became an icon, having won The Open in 1926, 1927 and 1930. From left: the Rev. Dr W.E.K. Rankin (chaplain to the R&A), St Andrews Town Councillor James Thomson, and St Andrews Provost David Niven do the unveiling. Bobby had died the previous December.

■ The Open, 1978, with crowds moving around the course. The Old Course was, until the creation of the New Course in 1895, known merely as "the golfing grounds".

It is often said to be on common land, meaning anyone can go for a walk round the links – play, and etiquette, permitting. Officially the land is "owned" by the St Andrews Links Trust, formed in 1974.

The course is treated with great respect by all who set foot upon it.

45

46

■ With the greatest respect to every other course all around the world, there is nothing as prestigious in the game as winning The Open at The Old Course, St Andrews.

This is Seve Ballasteros kissing the Claret Jug in 1984.

Pre-1950s

GOLF, like everything else in the world, looks more and more different to modern eyes the further back in time you go. But then, equally, some things never change.

The aim of this book is to evoke nostalgia, a remembrance of the golf we saw in our younger days. It isn't intended to be a comprehensive, year-by-year historical account.

So this chapter gives just a flavour of the game before most of us were born.

Golf in Scotland was always a more working class-friendly sport than in other parts of the world. Acceptance and respect in most, though certainly not all, clubhouses in our wee country was as much to do with the score you recorded as the car you drove (or bus you took, or long walk you had) to get to the course.

This didn't solely apply to playing the game, it also meant that bigger, and more diverse, galleries came out to watch.

Ordinary Scotsmen and women had (and still do have) a deep knowledge of the game. So when the greats come to test themselves on the best courses in existence, there was and still is keen interest in how they fare.

■ **A young Henry Cotton at St Andrews in 1927. He would go on to win The Open in 1934, 1937 and 1948.**

IT is impossible to overestimate the part Bobby Jones played in the development of the game in the USA – and around the world.

Bobby is the game's one true immortal.

Born in Atlanta in 1902, he remained an amateur his entire career and was famously modest, charismatic – but possibly the most naturally gifted golfer ever to play the game.

He won the "Grand Slam" of Majors (as they were recognised at the time) in a single year, 1930. The only man ever to do so. He is also the only man to be given two ticker-tape parades through New York City.

Bobby remained a working lawyer throughout this incredible career.

Following his retirement from playing he bought the land (for $70,000) and co-designed what would

become the Augusta National course and founded the Augusta Masters Tournament that would evolve to become a Major.

From 1948, however, Jones developed an extremely painful spinal condition that eventually confined him to a wheelchair and paralysed him.

He was named a Freeman of St Andrews in 1958 (see page 106). Bobby died, aged 69, in 1971.

■ **This photo shows the gallery following Bobby at St Andrews in 1927, on his way to a commanding six-shot victory and a second Claret Jug.**

1

2

3 ■ In the 1920s, as now, there was great interest in the swing of the greats. This 100-year-old newspaper sequence suggests that everyone could play like Bobby Jones if they just copied his swing. This might be something you've seen before – just substitute "Bobby Jones" with the name of whoever is the current world No. 1. **4**

■ Golf at Aberdour, circa 1900. Aberdour is a village in South Fife, overlooking the island of Inchcolm in the Firth of Forth. The abbey on the isle dates from 1235.

There are fantastic golf courses all around Scotland. Even the less-celebrated ones have lengthy and proud histories. And many – like Aberdour – have truly beautiful settings.

They are wonderful places to visit and to play a round.

■ **St Andrews at the turn of the 19th-20th Centuries.**

This photo has existed in a newspaper archive for more than 12 decades.

At some point, old-fashioned artist re-touching work has been done to suit some sports or news editor's whim.

The long grass by the pathway has been emphasised, and the flags atop buildings look rather too large and unnatural.

The skyline has also been painted over, possibly to hide high chimneys.

Shown at high-resolution, the ink-work, with brush or pen, and chinagraph pencil additions are easily seen. This was how photo enhancement was done in pre-digital days.

The photo is, however, for the most part a faithful representation of how the course and town looked in those days.

■ An even older photo: from 1891, before the Grand Hotel was built overlooking the 18th green. Work on it wasn't started until four years later.

The figure in the centre of the photo, facing the camera, is Old Tom Morris (1821-1908), the "grand old man of golf" – Open winner, course designer, club-maker, greenkeeper and golf administrator.

Image: JV-14165. Courtesy of the University of St Andrews Libraries and Museums

■ **Two photos of the British Amateur Championship of 1936, at the Old Course. This engine driver stopped while the players putted out on the 15th green. What matter train timetables when the title is at stake!**

Image: GMC-11-9-1. Courtesy of the University of St Andrews Libraries and Museums

■ Another photo of St Andrews' favourite adopted son, Bobby Jones, driving off the first. Despite the presence of the great man, that year's tournament would be won by Scotland's Hector Thomson.

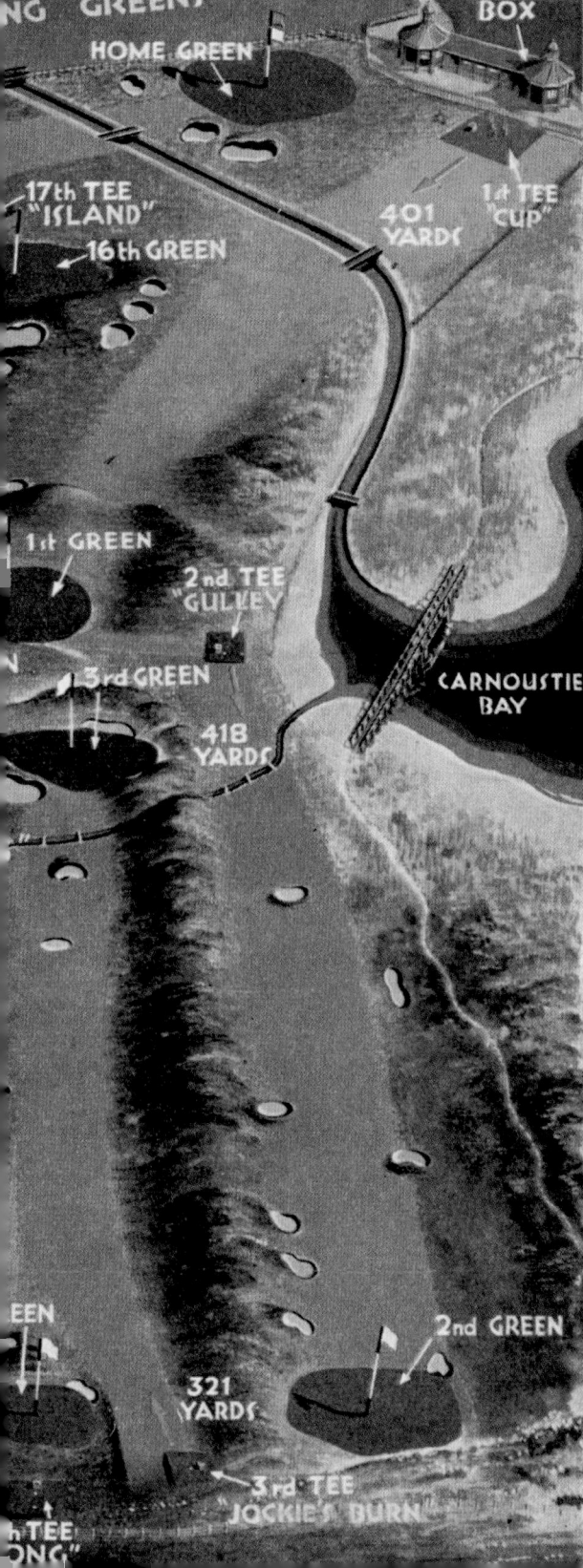

■ **This was an unusual publication for its day, though such things are common now.**

It was produced as promotional material by *The Evening Telegraph*, the local newspaper for Carnoustie, the venue for the 1937 Open – the second time (1931 being the first) it had been staged in Angus.

This map, if compared to today's course, shows there have been changes in the past decades. However, it doesn't fully illustrate how narrow and long the fairways at Carnoustie are.

And the formidable final three holes – the toughest test in Open golf – look almost pretty!

See also the Carnasty chapter on page 170.

64

■ **Carnoustie readies itself for the 1937 Open mentioned on the previous page.**

This, the second time the tournament had been played at the famous Angus links, was a star-studded affair.

All 11 members of the American Ryder Cup team who had competed (and won) at Southport two weeks previously stayed on to take part.

But the home-grown (or at least English) Henry Cotton beat them all to take the second of his three Claret Jugs.

The '37 Open was, however, what everyone likes to euphemistically refer to as "a true test of Scottish links golf". In other words, it absolutely poured with rain the entire time. Every player's four-round score was higher than par, Cotton's winning total being +2.

■ Carry your clubs, sir? St Andrews caddies pictured (from left) in about 1856, in 1924, and in 1939. The fashions (apart from the ubiquitous bunnets) might have changed, as have the types of bags (or use of bags in the first place) and the engineering of golf clubs. But the value of a knowledgeable and trustworthy caddy – who has a few secrets kept up his sleeve – has not. An experienced Old Course caddy can tell you exactly which club to select, and what to do with it, which is invaluable when you find yourself in the Valley of Sin . . . and with everyone watching (because there's always people hanging about around the 18th green) you really want to get up and down in two.

■ A partially light-damaged photo from 1931, the first time The Open was held at Carnoustie. A suitably-kilted Tommy Armour is given the trophy and a winner's cheque for £100. Edinburgh-born Tommy had a difficult time in World War One. He was temporarily blinded (it lasted several months) in one eye by the blast of a mustard gas shell, and had metal plates inserted in his skull and left arm. It was a wonder he ever managed to return to golf at all. He later became a US citizen and coached Babe Zaharias (see page 132). His 1953 *How To Play Your Best Golf All The Time* was for many years the best-selling book about golf.

■ Bobby Locke in 1939 at St Andrews. This would be the last Open for seven years. Champion was Englishman Dick Burton, ahead of American Johnny Bulla – the unluckiest man in golf. In that 1939 Open, on a miserably wet day, Bulla was the leader in the clubhouse but had to watch as Burton beat him with a famous birdie on the 18th. It would be the last Open for seven years.

■ The first post-war Open, again at St Andrews, and Johnny was runner-up again. He is seen congratulating winner Sam Snead. Who knows how many Majors Bulla might have won but for the war. With wartime restrictions still in place, only 100 qualifiers played the 1946 tournament and only 40 made the cut for the final day's morning and afternoon rounds. Play that day was made very difficult by strong winds, with every man in the top 10 recording over-par scores. It was Sam's only Open win. Johnny never did win a Major.

70

■ **The scoreboard, early on the first day of play, at the 1946 St Andrews Open.**

The operation of a scoreboard in the old days was a very different proposition to the press-of-a-button electronic and video screens of today.

News of what was happening, and who had scored what out on the course, was brought by runners. This information was then posted up.

Some scoreboards (see page 313) had the figures laboriously painted on by sign-writers.

Small boys in short trousers don't gather to comment, criticise and question the work of the modern scoreboard operator.

72

■ **The 1946 Open again.**

This shot, from this angle, of the 17th (the Road Hole) green at St Andrews is one of the most-often seen vintage views of the Old Course.

You will find many similar photos, of various tournaments, from down the years – indeed, you'll find another couple later in this book.

But only if they were taken before the late-1960s, when the footbridge at St Andrews Links Station (from where they were all shot) was closed.

The rail line curved away out of sight to the right.

Note the complete lack of any barrier to prevent spectators walking on to the course from the public road.

■ 1938. Francis Ouimet (right), non-playing captain of the American team, hands over the Walker Cup to John Beck, captain of the GB&I team at St Andrews. This was the first time the Brits (and Irish) had won the trophy – at the 10th time of asking – triumphing 7½ to 4½. Though to be accurate, half points weren't actually recorded in the scores until 1971. Ouimet would become the first American captain of the R&A.

■ The old clubhouse and starter's box behind the first tee at Carnoustie, as it was in 1947. This was the British Amateur Championship and would be won by Willie Turnesa. The American was also twice US Amateur champion and the youngest of a family of seven brothers – six of whom, Phil, Frank, Joe, Mike, Doug and Jim, became professional golfers. Willie was the only one who didn't ever turn pro.

■ **There have been a surprising number of parent-and-offspring Scottish golf stars.**

The most successful are Old Tom and Young Tom Morris, with eight Open championships between them. Willie Park Senior and Junior won a combined six Opens. With Willie Senior's brother Mungo also winning an Open.

John Panton is pictured on the right, elsewhere in this book you will find his daughter Cathy.

Colin Montgomerie's father James was secretary of Royal Troon.

Percy and Peter Alliss were also very successful golfers.

Pictured left are Laurie Ayton Senior and Junior in a 1945 photo. They are the grandson and great-grandson of William Ayton who, in 1843, was one of the 11 founder members of St Andrews Golf Club.

Not to break the line, David Ayton (Laurie Senior's father and William's son) recorded three top-10 finishes in The Open in the late 19th Century.

It's a family game.

Image: GMC-1-44-13. Courtesy of the University of St Andrews Libraries and Museums

■ John Panton, seen here (left) age 19 in 1935, after beating W. A. McKenzie in the Pitlochry Club Championship. John would go on to be one of the greats of Scottish golf – indeed he was so good they named a drink after him!

78

■ **The starter's box and clubhouses at Monifieth Links in 1949. It hasn't changed much.**

Image: JV-B-1467. Courtesy of the University of St Andrews Libraries and Museums

The 1950s

■ Bobby Locke on the 18th at St Andrews, on his way to winning the 1957 Open.

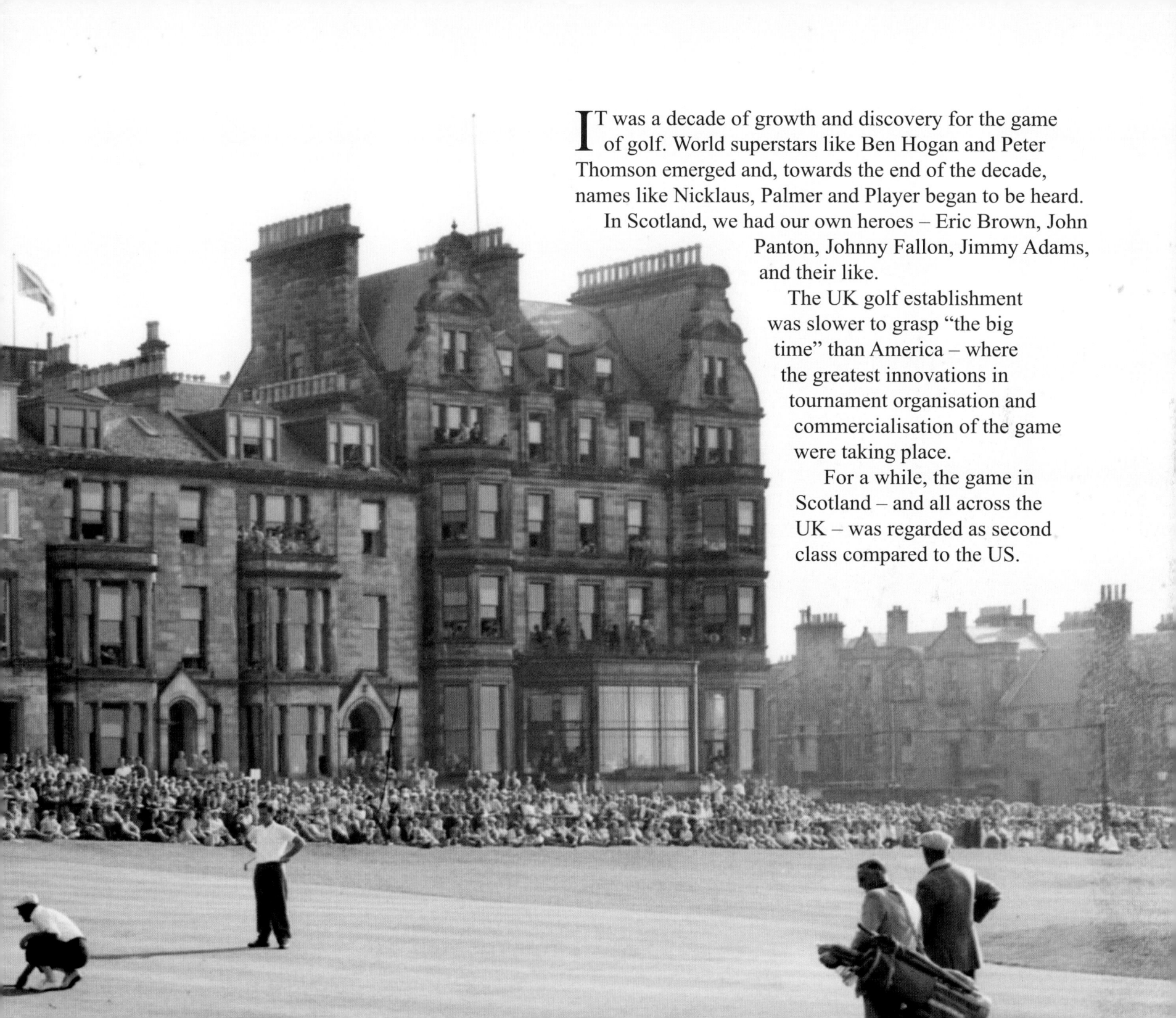

IT was a decade of growth and discovery for the game of golf. World superstars like Ben Hogan and Peter Thomson emerged and, towards the end of the decade, names like Nicklaus, Palmer and Player began to be heard. In Scotland, we had our own heroes – Eric Brown, John Panton, Johnny Fallon, Jimmy Adams, and their like.

The UK golf establishment was slower to grasp "the big time" than America – where the greatest innovations in tournament organisation and commercialisation of the game were taking place.

For a while, the game in Scotland – and all across the UK – was regarded as second class compared to the US.

TO younger golf fans, the idea of UK stars being properly full-time professional players, and a healthy European circuit of tournaments, must seem the norm. As if it has always been so.

But it hasn't always been so.

Golf in Britain in the 1950s was very different to today, and also very different to what was going on in America. The prize money for The Open was paltry compared to the riches on the American PGA Tour. The cut-throat level of competition was also a world away from the more genteel, polite atmosphere of golf in Scotland.

To illustrate just how marked this was, there is no better way than recalling the thoughts of one of the greats of the day who, from personal experience, knew what he was talking about.

The following is the opinion of Peter Thomson, the Australian five-time Open champion. He also competed on the PGA Tour.

He was writing for Scottish newspapers just before the 1957 Open, which is pictured on the previous page. In his words:

I THINK it is a great pity Britain doesn't have a full golf circuit as in America. On the US circuit there isn't a week without a tournament from January to September. Most are 72-hole stroke events.

The top names in golf are valuable for endorsing watches, clothing, whisky and cigarettes.

But the enthusiasm for watching golf here — particularly in Scotland — is greater than anywhere else in the world.

It seems logical that, with such terrific enthusiasm, efficiently-run tournaments would have a wide appeal throughout most of the year.

And such a circuit would throw up a home British player capable of taking on the world's best — yes, any American — and winning. As it is now, British players, highly talented though they are, divide their time between selling golf equipment, teaching, and occasionally playing in a tournament for prize money.

This is where they are at a terrific disadvantage in the big tournaments. Such as The Open at St Andrews, or any one of a dozen big-money events abroad.

Britain has a number of fine young tournament players. At the top of the list I place Peter Alliss and Bernard Hunt.

But I fear their golf potential will be wasted if they choose to follow the steadier and quieter life of a club pro. The opportunity is there for Alliss and Hunt, just the same as it was for me.

There is no reason why they should not do as well as I have done. Provided they are prepared to live the life of world travellers.

Unless some of the good young players in this country are prepared to follow this life — to live a hard, competitive tournament-after-tournament existence — then there's going to be a dearth of top-liners in Britain for years to come.

In fact, right now it is very hard to pick any British player at all who has more than an outside chance of winning at St Andrews this week.

And I have just told you why.

Few British players have even dared to attempt the highly competitive, tough tournaments of the US circuit. And none has ever done particularly well there.

Now, when these tournament-tested overseas players come to Britain they must have a terrific advantage. All the pre-tournament practice in the world cannot bring the home British player to the same pitch as those of us who have played tournaments every week for the past five months.

There's no greater sight in the golfing world than this great championship being played on the Old Course. As both Bobby Locke and I said at the presentation, what a great thing it would be if we played it there every year.

Permanent seating could be built. Grandstands at vantage points — say around the Loop or near the seventeenth. Permanent scoreboards could be erected along the course to the great satisfaction of all spectators. The difficulty in watching at St Andrews — as many of you found out — is trying to get to know what is going on in other parts of the course.

Walkie-talkie units at each green could flash scores

■ **Peter Thomson.**

to these boards and everyone could then follow the play, know the position — and sharpen the nerve-racking strain on the players fighting neck and neck.

It could be built up to out-do any of the mammoth American tourneys.

I'm all for having The Open at St Andrews every year. The course could be closed for a period before. And it could be coaxed into perfect condition.

I believe great players would come from far and wide to participate.

■ **The starter's hut and first tee at the 82nd Open, Carnoustie 1953.**

Total prize money that year was £2,500, an increase of 50% on 1952.

The winner's share was £500.

This was less than a third of the prize money available at that year's US Open.

Ben Hogan flew in to Scotland two weeks early, to practise with the smaller ball that was in use in Britain at the time.

All Majors were played with the same sized ball from 1974 onwards.

86

■ **The 1953 Open at Carnoustie again. This is the second green.**

A large gallery is seen following US star Lloyd Mangrum and celebrated local amateur David Hunter, of Monifieth.

Mangrum had won the 1946 US Open, and would tie for 24th place at this Open.

It wasn't the first time he'd been across the Atlantic, though. He had been among the American troops storming the Normandy beaches on D-Day.

Dubbed "Mr Icicle" by the press for his laid-back attitude, it probably was quite relaxing going for a stroll round a European seaside without members of the Wehrmacht trying to machine-gun him.

■ **The scoreboard at Carnoustie 1953.**

89

■ 1953 again. Ben Hogan after winning at Carnoustie.

Hogan, always described as one of the top three or four golfers of all time, only came over from the USA to play The Open on this single occasion.

Every time he played the course, he bettered his score, recording 73-71-70-68 over the four rounds. The last being a course record. That's some going on a links as demanding as Carnoustie.

In 2003, the 50th anniversary of that Open, Carnoustie's 6th hole was renamed Hogan's Alley in honour of the way Ben attacked it (and it is one of most difficult tests in world golf) in all four rounds in 1953.

It requires a steady nerve, and confidence in your accuracy, to drive for the narrow part of the fairway each time when there is so much at stake. It is a 23-yard landing strip. Then there is a second shot to a green that is guarded by three evil little bunkers. Hogan's famously reliable swing and distance-judgment didn't let him down.

■ Greats from closer to home at the 1953 Open. Scotland's Jimmy Adams and Englishman Dick Burton.

92

■ US President Dwight D. Eisenhower had a lifelong enthusiasm for golf in Scotland – particularly Turnberry. The Eisenhower Trophy (the World Amateur Team Championship) is named in his honour.

"Ike", as he was known, came to Turnberry in September 1959 when he was serving as president, and was surprised by how many people turned out to see him play.

He recorded an impressive birdie on the long 7th, but attributed his 18-over-par round to "nerves and rustiness".

■ Two shots of the crowds attracted to Carnoustie in 1953. This sort of eagerness to watch golf in Scotland in the 1950s set in motion the changes that came later. It was a slow progression, but any marketing man (not

that they were called that in those days) worth their salt could see there were commercial opportunities here. Golf clearly had the potential to be big business. All that was needed was imagination and hard work.

■ **On the road to . . . a game of golf in Scotland in the black and white era.**

Everyone loves golf. From ordinary Scots fowk to Hollywood's greatest stars.

This is Bob Hope (left) clowning with a caddy at Carnoustie in 1952, while Bing Crosby (right) visited St Andrews to take part in the first round of the British Amateur Golf tournament in 1950.

Playing under his real name, Harry Crosby, he was three up after three holes but eventually lost three-and-two to local builder James Wilson.

Bing and James remained friends and in 1972 set up the Bing Crosby Trophy for Royal & Ancient club members aged over 60.

Bing had been an R&A member since 1951.

Bob Hope attempted to play the 1951 British Amateur at Porthcawl but was eliminated in the first round of qualifying.

■ The 1955 Open at St Andrews.

American Cary Middlecoff blasts out of an Old Course bunker.

Note the debris on the surface and the grass growing through the sand. Bunkers are kept tidier these days.

Middlecoff won three Majors and went on to become the USA's version of Peter Alliss, a renowned TV commentator.

Cary was one of only five Americans in the field for that 1955 Open – and two of them were amateurs.

The top American pro to come over, Ed Furgol, was the reigning US Open champion, despite having one arm 10 inches shorter than the other.

■ **Bobby Locke is presented with the 1957 Claret Jug by Dr Gardner Hill, captain of the R&A.**

There was some controversy over this Open. On the last green of his final round Bobby moved his ball a putter-head length to the side to avoid the line of his playing partner, Bruce Crampton.

But Bobby forgot to move his ball back to its original position and sank a four-footer.

No one realised this for several hours, until (reportedly) second-placed Peter Thomson spotted it in the highlights that were shown on television that evening, long after the presentation shown on the left had taken place.

The Championship Committee ruled that no advantage had been gained, but it was said that relations between Thomson and Locke were irreparably damaged.

This was the first Open in which the leaders went off last in the final round. Previously, playing order for all rounds had been drawn by ballot.

■ **Gary Player shares a laugh with the crowd while waiting for the presentation ceremony to begin after winning The Open at Muirfield in 1959. The gentlemanly South African was always very popular with Scottish galleries.**

Image: GMC-7-32-11. Courtesy of the University of St Andrews Libraries and Museums

102 ■ The Walker Cup is played for by amateur golfers of the US and Great Britain & Ireland. It is named for George Walker, president of the USGA when the competition started in 1922. Walker was the grandfather of US President George H. Bush and great-grandfather of US President George W. Bush.

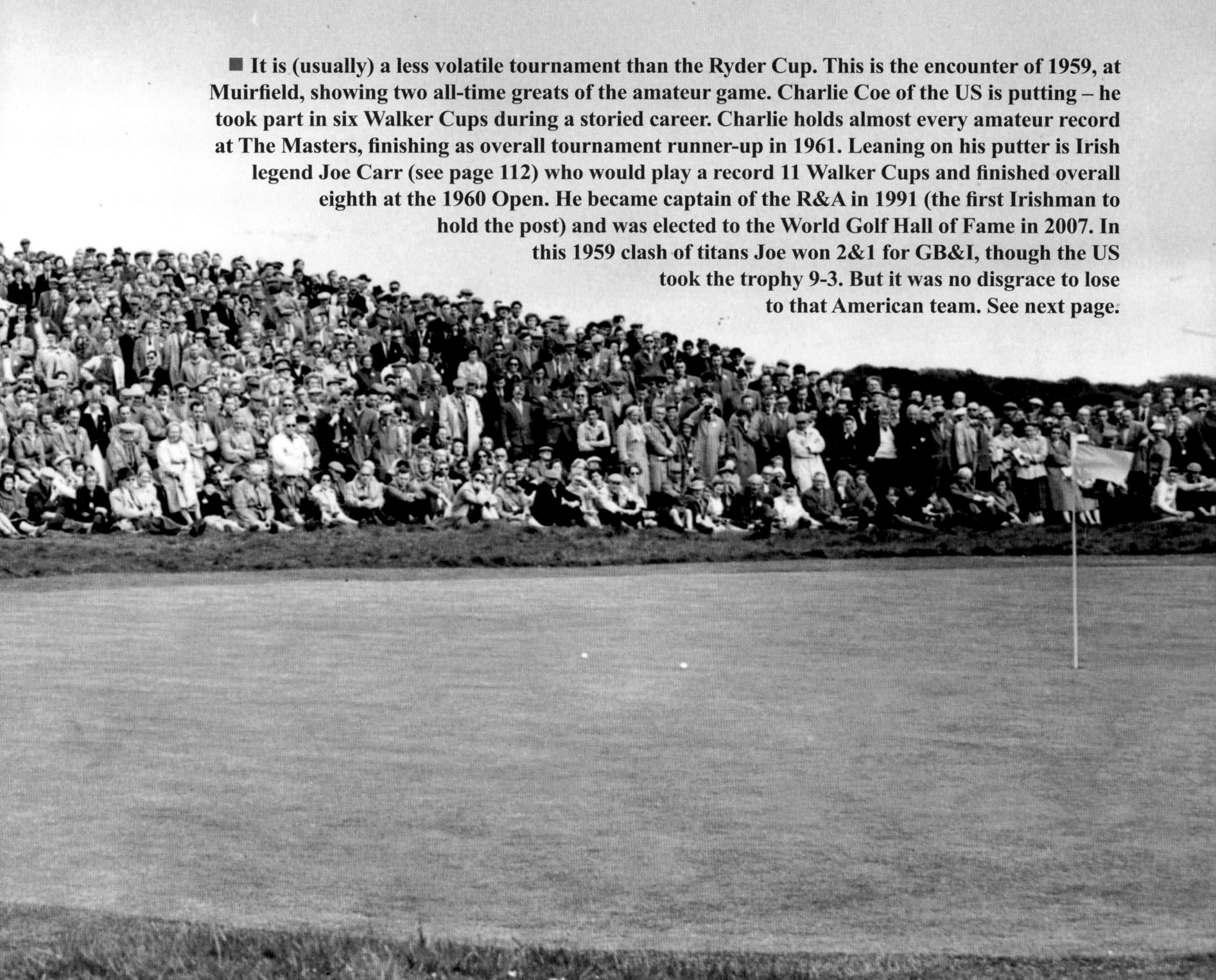

■ It is (usually) a less volatile tournament than the Ryder Cup. This is the encounter of 1959, at Muirfield, showing two all-time greats of the amateur game. Charlie Coe of the US is putting – he took part in six Walker Cups during a storied career. Charlie holds almost every amateur record at The Masters, finishing as overall tournament runner-up in 1961. Leaning on his putter is Irish legend Joe Carr (see page 112) who would play a record 11 Walker Cups and finished overall eighth at the 1960 Open. He became captain of the R&A in 1991 (the first Irishman to hold the post) and was elected to the World Golf Hall of Fame in 2007. In this 1959 clash of titans Joe won 2&1 for GB&I, though the US took the trophy 9-3. But it was no disgrace to lose to that American team. See next page.

THE photographs in this book are drawn from newspaper and magazine archives, where many of them endured a long working life in golf reportage.

This photo of the 1959 US Walker Cup team shows that sports and picture editors over the years have called for early shots of a young golfer. He has been cut out and given a whitened background for solo head-and-shoulders appearances in various publications.

That starlet was, of course, Jack Nicklaus. This trip to Scotland was the first time the 19-year-old pharmaceutical student had travelled overseas. He had never before played on a links course. Unsurprisingly, the up-and-coming superstar adapted instantly and performed admirably.

Nicklaus was a member of the Walker Cup teams of 1959 and 1961, winning all four of his matches. He had just become the youngest man since 1909 to win the US Amateur.

The rest of that 1959 US team were no duffers either. Each man was an accomplished, highly-decorated player. Apart from Nicklaus and Charlie Coe (mentioned on the previous page) the standouts were Tommy Aaron, who would win the 1973 Masters, and Deane Beman who was the US Open runner-up in 1969 before going on to become PGA Tour Commissioner for 20 years from 1974. That line-up has been called the best American Walker Cup team of all time.

When they reached Muirfield the four rookies – Nicklaus, Beman, Aaron and Wettlaufer – immediately went out to hit a few balls, accompanied by a few reporters and some Muirfield club members. It was quickly obvious that this was an incredible gathering of young talent.

In that practice round Nicklaus almost drove the green on the 11th, a 387-yard par 4. Legend has it that the newspapermen and locals turned back to the clubhouse at that point, to spread the bad news of these "Unbeatables".

■ **The 1959 US Walker Cup team. Back, from left: Tommy Aaron, Jack Nicklaus, Ward Wettlaufer, William Hyndman III.
Front: E. Harvie Ward Jr, Deane Beman, Charlie Coe (captain), William Patton, and Frank Taylor Jr.**

BOBBY JONES was perhaps the most influential man in the history of golf. And he grew to love St Andrews.

In turn, St Andrews loved him right back.

Though the great man's romance with the Old Course hadn't started well (see page 42) Bobby won The Open in 1927 and the British Amateur in 1930 at St Andrews.

After his 1927 victory (the second of his three Opens, he also won at Royal Lytham & St Annes in 1926, and Royal Liverpool in 1930) Bobby requested that the Claret Jug should "remain here in St Andrews with my friends at the Royal & Ancient" instead of taking it back to his home in Atlanta.

This mark of respect was just one of the gestures which so endeared him to the people of Fife.

In 1958 he was made a freeman of the city of St Andrews, and named an honorary burgess of the town. A burgess is an ancient title bestowed upon people who owned property in a city and who could, therefore, expect its protection. The effect of the honorary title is very much like saying, "By legal right, you are now a citizen of our town."

Bobby was, by that time, badly affected by the spinal condition that eventually ended his life.

After the investiture, the crowd who had gathered both inside and outside the Younger Hall sang *For He's A Jolly Good Fellow*, then the old Scottish air *Will Ye No Come Back Again*, a song of fond farewell, which should be taken as a great distinction by any man.

The previous American granted the freedom of St Andrews was Benjamin Franklin, in 1759. The next would be Jack Nicklaus in 2022.

There is no higher honour for a golfer.

■ Above: Bobby shakes hands with St Andrews Provost Robert Leonard in The Younger Hall at The University of St Andrews during the Freedom of the City ceremony on the evening of October 9th, 1958.
■ Left: a close-up of the scroll given to Bobby. It details the town's thanks for Bobby's part in setting up the Eisenhower Trophy, the first instalment of which was being played on the Old Course that week.

■ Golf in Scotland isn't just about the top pros and Open winners. There is a thriving amateur and weekend golfing tradition that goes back hundreds of years. This is an important aspect of golf in our country. There have been many accomplished players who deserve to be celebrated. Some (such as John Panton) became successful professionals. Others remained amateur but were hugely respected in their clubs. Even years after their best achievements they would be acknowledged in their communities (even by those who didn't play the game) as "a braw golfer". Above is Reid Jack, the 1955 Scottish and 1957 British Amateur champion.

■ From left: David Allan, Fred Bullock, John Panton and Alex Deboys before their match in the 1955 Scottish pro-am foursomes at Pollock. Alex and Fred beat John and David on this occasion. All of them, though some are perhaps not household names today, were very well-known golfers.

■ This is the vast gallery watching the 1956 British Amateur Championship at Royal Troon. England's John Beharrel had just sunk a long putt to beat Scotland's Les Taylor. Beharrel, at 18, was at that time the youngest ever winner of the "British". He was captain of the R&A in 1998.

■ A closer look at Joe Carr, one of the greats of the 1950s. His swing was said to be a model of grace and beauty. This photo looks like it could be a publicity shot from a Hollywood blockbuster about golf!

■ Scotland's Johnny Fallon doesn't get as much attention as his career deserves. Born in 1913, the Second World War interrupted his best years. He tied third at the 1939 Open and was runner-up in 1955. Johnny, a Lanark lad, played on the 1955 Ryder Cup team and was non-playing captain in 1963.

Irons ladies

SCOTTISH women have a long and proud record in the history of golf.

Though it hasn't been easy.

To say that there wasn't much of an "inclusive culture" in the black and white era is putting it mildly.

However, many gifted female golfers have strode Scotland's fairways.

The British Ladies Amateur was established in 1893, the Scottish Women's Amateur Championship was first played in 1903. These were, until the dawn of the professional era, the leading competitions for ladies.

Both are match play, and to win required the stamina to play the semi-final and final on the same day.

This chapter will highlight just a few of the ladies who won those tournaments, or were very highly regarded in the game.

Sad to say, however, there just weren't so many photos taken of the women's game. It hasn't been easy to find images of many who deserve to be featured here.

My apologies for the lack of attention photographers gave to the women's game in the past.

■ The photo on the left shows Jessie Valentine, before her marriage, playing in a Scottish Women's Foursome Championship at North Berwick.

■ Right, Jessie with the Scottish Ladies Amateur trophy, after winning it for the second year in succession in 1939.

She was known to many, very affectionately, as Wee Jessie.

Born in Perth in 1915, her father, Joe Anderson, played cricket for Scotland and was the golf pro at the Craigie Hill club in the town.

Jessie's career started early and was littered with silverware.

She won the Girls Amateur Championships in 1933, then the British Ladies Amateur three times, and Scottish Ladies Amateur six times between 1937 and 1958 – despite not playing during the war.

She also won the New Zealand and French Women's Opens and appeared in the Curtis Cup seven times (a sequence again affected by the war).

She was awarded an MBE in 1959, and inducted into the Scottish Sports Hall of Fame in 2003.

Wee Jessie, a giant of the game, died in 2006, age 91.

■ Jessie Valentine at Carnoustie in 1961, having (just) carried the Barry Burn. It looks like a tricky lie, but no problem for the deft Jessie.

■ **Two of the greats – Charlotte Beddows and Jean Anderson during the "British" at St Andrews in 1965. Jean won the Scottish title three times, 1947, 1949, and 1952, playing as Jean Donald.**

■ **Left:** The redoubtable Charlotte Beddows walks over the Swilken Burn in 1961, during the Scottish Amateur.

She is playing against Mrs Jean Lawson, of Carnoustie, who is alongside her.

Charlotte was a great hero of Scottish golf. She was born in 1887 (which means she is aged 73 in this photo – but still competing).

■ **Right:** Charlotte in bunker trouble at St Andrews, six years later in 1967 – at the remarkable age of 79.

This was a full 47 years after winning her first Scottish title.

Charlotte, who was often referred to very respectfully as "Mrs Beddows", was four times Scottish champion and played in the first Curtis Cup in 1932.

She also captained Scotland's hockey team in her teenage years.

Charlotte died in 1976, aged 88.

■ **Helen Holm, a Scottish golfing legend, with the Scottish Ladies Amateur trophy of 1950.**

Born Helen Gray in Partick, Glasgow, in 1907, she had a lengthy and highly successful career.

Helen won the 1928 Lanarkshire Open, and played at the pinnacle of the game for the next 30 years. She was Scottish Ladies champion five times, 1930, 1932, 1937, 1948, and 1950, and won the "British" twice, 1934 and 1938.

She reached the final of the Scottish on a further five occasions, the last being 1957.

She was on two Curtis Cup teams, 1938 and '48, but declined the chance to play in the 1950 tournament in the US as she didn't want to leave her young son.

The Helen Holm Scottish Women's Open is named after her, and the uniquely-shaped trophy is made from her wooden-shafted jigger (wedge) and some of her medals.

■ **Marigold Speir with the 1957 Scottish Ladies Amateur trophy after winning at Troon.**

Marigold was a resident of St Andrews and beat Helen Holm in that 1957 final.

She represented GB&I in the Vagliano Trophy, as well as her country in several Home International matches – captaining the Scottish team in 1971. She went on to be a Scottish selector.

She was twice captain of the St Rule Club in St Andrews, and also president.

Marigold became a well-known and greatly respected figure in St Andrews, generously giving her time to several charities.

She died in 2015, aged 80.

■ **Left, Marley Spearman with the British Woman's Amateur Championship trophy she won at Carnoustie in 1961.**

Marley was English, but her unusual route into golf made her very famous in the 1960s.

She had been a professional dancer on the West End stage. One day caught in a rainstorm while shopping at Harrods, and unable to find a cab, she spotted a sign offering golf lessons and thought to fill in half an hour.

When the pro giving the lessons spotted her natural athleticism and graceful swing, he recommended she take up the game.

She had her handicap down to four within two years, and went on to win the British championship twice and the English once, as well as the Commonwealth title and play in four Curtis Cup teams.

■ **Right, Ann Irvin lifts the British Women's Amateur Championship trophy, at Carnoustie, in 1973.**

Ann was another English (Lytham St Annes) winner of the 'British' at Carnoustie.

She also won the English Championship twice, played on four Curtis Cup teams, and in eight Vagliano Trophy matches against the Europeans.

She went on to become English Women's Golf Association president, and was appointed an MBE in 2011 for services to golf.

■ **Possibly the best, certainly the most successful, Scottish golfer of all time is Belle Robertson.**

Isabella McCorkindale was born in 1936 and won the Scottish Women's Amateur on seven occasions, the most by any golfer.

She was victorious in 1965, 1966, 1971, 1972, 1978, 1980, and 1986.

She reached the final of the "British" on three occasions: in 1959 (as Belle McCorkindale), 1965 and 1970, each time ending the tournament as the beaten finalist, before at last taking the title herself at Conwy, Wales, in 1981.

She represented UK&I in the Curtis Cup nine times, twice as non-playing captain, winning the cup on the last of those occasions in 1986 at the Prairie Dunes Country Club, Kansas, by a score of 13-5.

She also won the Helen Holm trophy three times

and was British Stroke-play champion three times.

Belle was a great believer in physical fitness, keeping herself supple and strong throughout her career.

This helped greatly with her powerful striking off the tee.

She was inducted into the Scottish Sports Hall of Fame in 2002, after being voted Scottish Sportswoman of the Year on four occasions.

Belle was made an MBE in 1973.

In 2015 she became one of the first female honorary members, along with Princess Anne, of the R&A.

■ **Belle is pictured, left, in 1960 (you can see the natural grace and athleticism in her stance) and right, addressing the ball in 1973.**

■ Belle Robertson (left) in 1980, giving us a good look at the trophy as she takes her sixth Scottish title at Carnoustie, after a dramatic last-hole win over Perth's Fiona Anderson.

■ Right: A young Belle in 1965 with Brigitte Varangot when Belle was runner-up to the great French player in the "British" at St Andrews.

■ **Left: Moira Paterson (who would become Moira Milton in 1953) pictured in 1948.**

Moira, born in Castle Douglas, Galloway, but raised in Lenzie, was another fierce competitor in the years following the war.

She won the British Ladies Amateur at Troon in 1952 – a real battle with England's Bunty Stephens.

Moira was then runner-up to Helen Holm in the Scottish, also in 1952.

Later that year she was in the GB&I Curtis Cup team that beat the Americans 5-4 at Muirfield.

For much of her career she worked as a gym teacher.

■ **Right:** Moving closer to the modern era, this is Cathy Panton (daughter of the renowned John Panton) pictured in 1973. She clearly had a flair for golf.

Showing an aptitude for the game to match her dad, Cathy had just turned 19 when she won the British Ladies Amateur in 1976.

She was then voted Scottish Sportswoman of the Year.

Unlike most of the other ladies in this chapter, Cathy was able to turn pro in 1978 as a founding member of the Ladies European Tour.

Indeed, she topped the Women's Professional Golf Association's (as it was then known) Order of Merit in its inaugural season.

Cathy's earnings that first year were £4,965, but the LET has gone from strength to strength since those early days.

The modern tour, with total prize money of around £18m per year, owes much to its pioneers.

Cathy went on to record 14 wins between 1979 and 1988 and is still tied for 7th most wins on the tour.

■ **Joan Lawrence during the Scottish Amateur at Troon, 1957, having just given her ball a "good skite" (as we say in Scotland).**

Joan would go on to win three Scottish titles in a row, 1962, '63 and '64, and reach the 1965 final, only to lose to upcoming young star Belle Robertson.

Joan was also the Fife Ladies champion an astonishing 18 times.

She would later have a long career as an organiser, administrator and international team selector, and was chairman of the Ladies Golf Union and president of the Scottish Ladies Golfing Association.

Joan was awarded an MBE in 1999 for services to ladies' amateur golf.

Another giant of the game in Scotland.

The legend that was Babe Zaharias

THE greatest female athlete, and possibly the best golfer, who ever lived was Babe Zaharias.

Born Mildred Didriksen in Texas in 1911, she was a one-off. Nothing seemed beyond her sporting prowess. She was an All-American basketball player, and also excelled at baseball, roller-skating, tennis, ice-hockey, diving, boxing, and 10-pin bowling. She also made all her own clothes and found time to record hit 45s for Mercury Records.

Babe came to attention at the US Amateur Athletic Union Olympic tryouts in 1932, age 21. She competed in eight events, winning six of them, inside three hours. She set three world records that day, in the javelin, baseball throw, and high jump.

Later that year she set a further four world records at the Los Angeles Olympics, winning gold in the hurdles sprint, javelin, and a high jump silver (though she matched the best height).

She didn't have a coach, or any help. She trained herself.

Then she took up golf in 1935 and, at first forced to remain amateur as there was no pro women's game, dominated the sport for almost two decades. At one point she won 14 tournaments in a row, and won 82 in total.

She developed colon cancer, aged 42, in 1953, but continued to play golf almost up until her last week. She won the 1954 US Women's Open by 12 shots, a month after undergoing a colostomy. When she died, in September 1956, she was still ranked World No.1 woman golfer.

"The Babe" visited Scotland in 1947 and was a media sensation. We had never seen anything like it (see next page).

Image: GMC-2-42-2. Courtesy of the University of St Andrews Libraries and Museums

Babe came to Gullane to contest the 1947 British Amateur. No American lady amateur had ever won "The British" in its 54-year history.

Never a shy person, Babe couldn't work out why Scottish galleries were so quiet and respectful. As she went round the course she chatted to the spectators urging them to make more noise.

However, never having experienced rough as thick as that at Gullane, she arrived several days early and went out and practised hitting through it. Swinging into a particularly wet and tangled tuft she jarred herself so badly that she chipped a bone in her thumb. However, she hid this from the press, as she didn't want to seem to have an "excuse ready" if she lost.

As she progressed through the tournament, Babe insisted on playing the by-holes, during which she would clown about, putting through her legs and playing trick shots. Scotland had never seen the like.

Publicity said she stood six feet three – though she doesn't look quite that tall in these photos. Her height was perhaps exaggerated to add to her Amazonian reputation.

It was her length off the tee that really wowed. The newspapers described her as "spectacular" and "a phenomenon".

Asked by reporters for the secret of her long hitting, she quipped, "I just loosen my girdle and let the ball have it." This was reported in many newspapers, causing outrage in some quarters at such vulgar talk.

Babe kept winning. From an initial field of 99 she made it through the match-play rounds to the semi-final where she met the formidable Jean Donald.

Image: GMC-2-42-4. Courtesy of the University of St Andrews Libraries and Museums

This was the match-up everyone had been waiting for. Jean was the reigning Scottish champion, a superb golfer in her own right (she is pictured on page 117).

Jean possessed a fierce competitiveness. But Babe won seven-and-five, shooting one under men's par, then beat England's Jacqueline Gordon four-and-three to take the title.

She treated the crowd to an impromptu Highland Fling during the awards ceremony and sung a Scottish song. If it all sounds a little unusual – it certainly was – but the public loved this Texan whirlwind.

Babe went on to try several other Scottish courses over the next four days. All three photos in this book are from her visit to The Old Course.

She clowned and played to the galleries on this short tour of the nation's great golfing venues. One of her favourite tricks was to tee her ball quite low and surreptitiously place a match behind it, half pushed into the grass.

When she hit the ball the match head (caught between club face and ball) cracked like a rifle shot and a puff of smoke was created – it was quite a surprise and an arresting piece of theatre for those who had never seen such a thing done before.

Everywhere she went, the crowds flocked to see her.

Around 1,000 (including a high proportion of women) turned up at St Andrews.

The original plan had been for a quiet visit, with no spectators allowed. But Babe saw the huge gathering behind the fence at the first tee and waved them all on to the course to follow her, talking to and joking with them as she played.

Image: GMC-2-42-9. Courtesy of the University of St Andrews Libraries and Museums

St Andrews

ONE of the things that makes St Andrews different from almost all other "golf towns" across the world is that the famous Old Course starts and finishes within the town.

There is no car journey, or even much of a walk, to reach it. You just turn off North Street, go a short distance down Golf Place, and you are there. The Links is a street that runs alongside the 18th hole. Old Station Road goes alongside the 17th, out to The Jigger Inn.

All this seems normal to locals – it is, after all, the way it has been for half a millennium.

But to visitors and tourists used to golf courses situated at out-of-town country clubs or resorts, the sheer "ordinariness" can be quite startling.

In many ways St Andrews, and golf at St Andrews, are the same thing.

■ **Left: This ornate sign used to mark the boundary on the Anstruther Road – until it was stolen in 1961!**

■ **Right: Market Street, the centre of town, in 1973.**

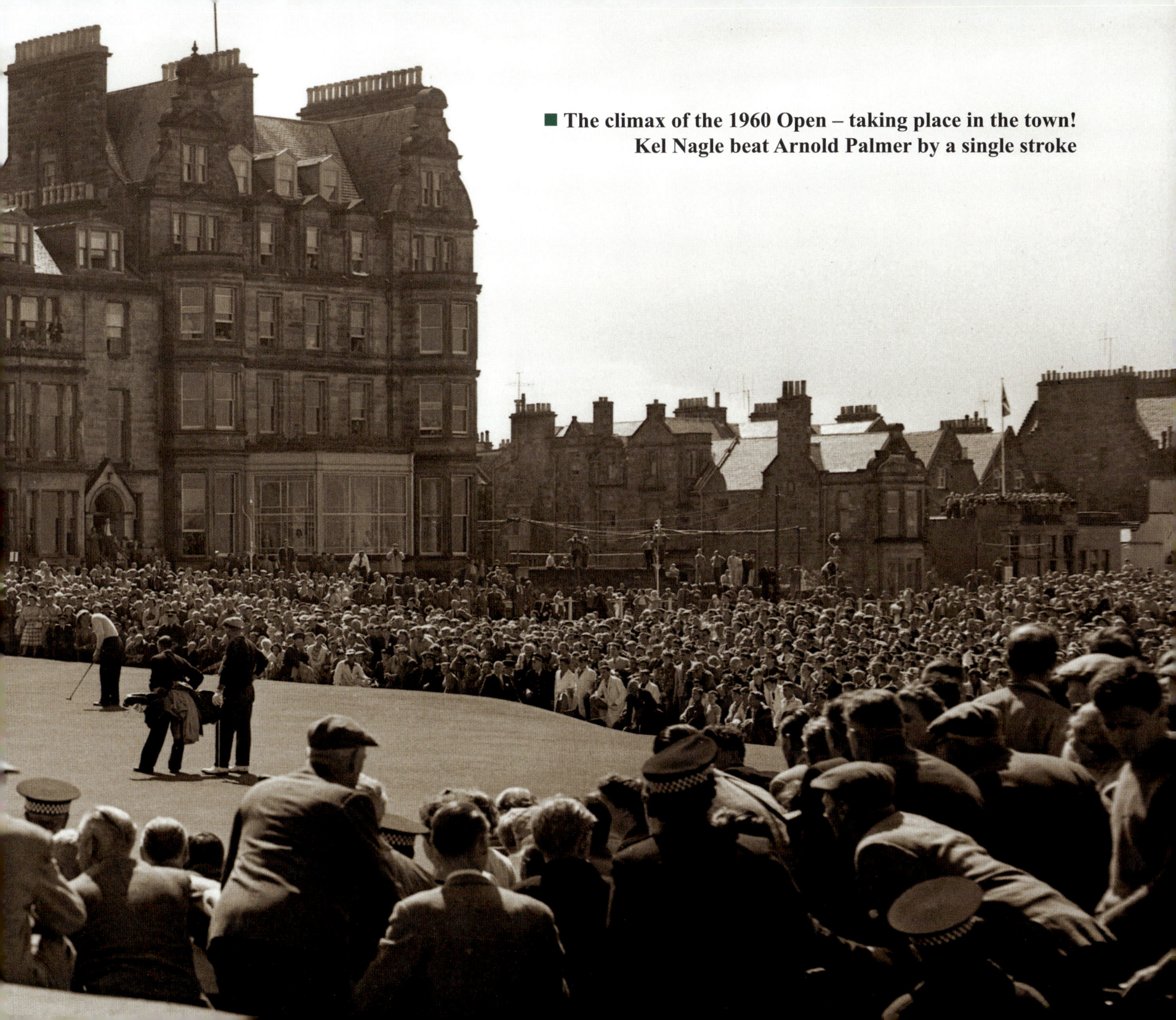

■ **The climax of the 1960 Open – taking place in the town! Kel Nagle beat Arnold Palmer by a single stroke**

■ The old St Andrews has three long streets at its heart – all visible in this aerial photo (although the plane wing slightly obscures North Street on the right). Market Street is in the middle, with South Street on the left. The town grew from the cathedral, which became the centre of religion in Scotland. The oldest church on the site is thought to have been founded in or around the year 345. St Regulas had a vision which led him to remove the bones of the Apostle Andrew from their resting place in Greece to the "western ends of the earth". In other words: Fife.

■ The ruins of St Andrews Cathedral and St Rule's Tower (on the left). This is the "new" cathedral, it replaced the older one that had been attached to the St Rule Tower. Building work on the replacement started in 1158. It was, in its heyday, the largest building in Europe. However, it was damaged during the Reformation in 1559 and fell into ruin. Much of the stone was carried away for other local buildings.

■ Everywhere you look in St Andrews the depth of history is apparent. A university founded in 1431 here, a 12th Century castle there. The above is Blackfriars Chapel, on South Street, which dates from the mid-15th Century (this photo was taken on April 13th, 1932).

These ancient buildings are scattered through the town. Walking past 1,700 years of history on your way to the shops is just part and parcel of living in St Andrews.

■ The Jigger Inn, arguably the most famous 19th hole in golf, pictured in 1976. It was built in the 1850s as the station master's house when the railway reached St Andrews, and is very close to the infamous Road Hole on the Old Course. "Jigger" is either (depending on who you believe, and how sober you think they are) an old type of golf club with a shortened staff, or a stick for measuring out alcohol.

■ St Andrews in 1954, from the west (this page) with the Old Course in view, and east (opposite) from the harbour side, with the ruins of the cathedral. It is a golf town, but also much more.

■ Left: Bringing in the harvest in the 1950s, with the ruins of the Cathedral in the background. St Andrews is a rural town, with rich countryside on all of its landward edges.

■ Above, caravans at Kinkell Braes in 1954, with St Andrews East Sands in the background. There is still a caravan park in this area, though it now has the Castle Course (opened in 2008) close behind it.

150

■ **The West Sands stretch alongside the Old Course and are, like the links, public land that anyone can enjoy. The Old Course is behind the dunes to the right.**

This pic shows locals taking advantage of a rare sunny and not-too-windy day in the summer of 1983.

The West Sands famously played the part of Broadstairs Beach in Kent in the 1981 multiple Oscar-winning movie *Chariots of Fire*.

It was generally agreed that they gave a very convincing performance, though the Hamilton Grand building and St Rules Tower can be clearly seen towards the end of the running-on-the-beach sequence in the film!

■ Another resulting quirk of the golf course being on public land and, essentially, inside the town, is that a public road, Granny Clark's Wynd, traverses the 1st and 18th fairways (these things must seem odd to Americans used to private courses like Augusta National). To minimise injury and (worse) interference with approach shots, a traffic light system was put up in the late 1960s; though it has since been removed.

■ Quaint days that will never be seen again. The leaderboard behind the clubhouse during The Open of 1955. The leaderboard isn't on the course, it is in the town – roughly where the R&A World Golf Museum is now.

■ The Old Course, as seen from the 570-year-old bell tower of St Salvator's Chapel, in 1970.

■ Friday, July 14th, 1978. Jack Nicklaus would battle his way to a third Open win, clinched with a 69 to hold off the challenges of Ray Floyd, Tom Kite and Ben Crenshaw. It was a great Open. This was the scene looking down The Links, which runs alongside the 18th fairway of the Old Course. A major golf event is taking place, but the road (separated from the course by a low fence) had to remain open for access to the private houses that line the street. Another example of St Andrews (the town) and St Andrews (the world-renowned sporting venue) existing comfortably and unfussily alongside each other.

156

■ **The 17th (The Road Hole) on the Old Course is called that because it is, simply, next to a public thoroughfare (Old Station Road).**

A wayward approach shot can be expensive (the complexities of your first and second shots on the 17th are outlined on pages 40 and 41).

This is Dumbarton's Charlie Green playing for GB & Ireland against John Grace of the USA in the 1975 Walker Cup.

He is aiming a chip towards the green from a hard lie in the middle of the road. Not the first, or the last, golfer who has found themselves in this position.

Often, shots that roll on to the road here will trundle up close to the limestone wall on the other side – leaving very little room to swing.

The traditional remedy for this (local worthies will tell you) is to hit towards the wall, judging the bounce and rebound speed just right to go pin-high.

Sounds easy if you say it fast!

The GB&I team was: David Marsh (captain), John Davies, Richard Eyles, Charlie Green, Peter Hedges, Ian Hutcheon, Mark James, George Macgregor, Pat Mulcare, Martin Poxon and Hugh Stuart.

The US team was: Ed Updegraff (captain), George Burns, William C. Campbell, Vinny Giles, John Grace, Jay Haas, Gary Koch, Jerry Pate, Dick Siderowf, Craig Stadler and Curtis Strange.

The American amateurs won the tournament 15½ to 8½.

■ **The 1st and 18th holes of the Old Course sit in an arena formed by St Andrews buildings that have become famous over the years.**

Left is the Grand Hotel, pictured in 1949.

It was built in 1895 by businessman Thomas Hamilton, the first hotel in Scotland to have hot and cold running water in every room.

It was an RAF training HQ during the war, then became student halls of residence.

It is now an upmarket apartment complex known as the Hamilton Grand.

Right is another oft-photographed building. This 1951 photo shows it as The Marine Hotel. It was opened in 1887 and had various owners.

It is now the very well-regarded Rusacks Hotel, and has been greatly extended and improved in recent years.

■ **St Andrews townsfolk in (and on top of) their iconic buildings watch their game being played on their course. This was The Open of 1978.**

CAPTAINS of the R&A traditionally take part in a driving-in ceremony to mark the beginning of their term in office.

They serve for one year at a time in an ambassadorial role, representing the R&A at championships and in the organisation's efforts to develop the game of golf.

The captain plays in with a tee shot from the 1st, which is pursued by the caddies. The captain then "buys back" his ball with a reward of a gold sovereign.

To mark the early-morning ceremony, which is always very well attended, a cannon is fired – just as the drive is made.

The ceremony symbolises the days when the captain was whoever won the Silver Club competition among members, though it has been an elected office since 1806.

In essence, the elected captain still "plays", though he is the only person in the competition.

The cannon is said to be a relic from a Crimean War-era supply ship, HMS Sutlej, wrecked in St Andrews Bay in 1856.

■ **Above:** Captain Provost W. Norman Boase plays his way into office in 1935, with the cannon just having gone off in an impressive puff of smoke in the background.
■ **Left:** Head greenkeeper Andrew Nicoll preparing to fire the cannon in 1958.

■ The quiet times. An Open at St Andrews is the greatest, most prestigious golf event in existence, but the town carries on in its own unhurried way when there isn't a world-famous tournament taking place. Many would say the quiet times are the best time to visit, as that's when the true atmosphere of St Andrews can be felt. And it is, indeed, difficult to understand and appreciate the depth of history when all the razzmatazz is taking place. These photos show the R&A clubhouse in 1979 (above) and, from another angle, in 1969 (right).

166

■ The Old Course greenkeeping staff line up with their equipment (which has clearly been "shined up" for the occasion) for an early-morning photo before the start of the 1962 golf season.

Greenkeepers rarely get the recognition they deserve, but course management is an incredibly important part of the workings of any club.

It isn't easy to get all the greens to run at the same rate, or keep the fairways divot-free, or the rough at just the right length, or any one of the thousand and one other things they do.

A good greenkeeper has to have a "feel" for the turf. It's an intuitive, almost mystical, thing. The more years of experience you have, the better you are at it.

It's also a life of long hours, early starts (especially in the summer months), heavy work . . . and not many greenkeepers ever owned Ferraris!

In those days all of them would have lived in, or very close to, the town.

They were all proud St Andrews men.

■ This is the view of St Andrews that golfers see when they are coming down the 18th, nearing the end of their round. It is a beautiful view, full of character... and yet for a player it is also quite daunting. In a highly-pressured match about to reach a conclusion it takes a strong-minded golfer to remember to play the hole, not the history.

This is The Open of 1984.

■ Above: Henry Cotton who won the second of his three Opens at Carnoustie in 1937, delivers a talk at Carnoustie Golf Club in 1950.

Carnasty

THERE is a fervent passion for golf in the Angus town of Carnoustie.

The roots go back almost as far as those of St Andrews just a few miles away across the Tay estuary. There are records of golf on the links from the 16th Century.

The town is fiercely proud of its links, branded "Car-nasty" by traumatised visiting players. It is the most difficult course on the Open rota.

And it lives up to that reputation.

The length – 7,421 yards – is the longest of any Open course. But it is the narrow fairways that supply the real test. Even a slightly wayward drive can land you in jungle-standard rough.

Add an exposed aspect that leaves it at the mercy of the North Sea wind – which always seems to come in gusts – and you have a test of golf that is daunting to all but the very best.

The locals love all this. They will tell you that anyone who conquers Carnoustie must be a REAL golfer.

■ Right: Carnoustie High Street in 1948. Like St Andrews, the first tee of the golf course (though not visible here) is situated almost within the town itself.

■ The tented village at Carnoustie, 1953.

Despite what people may say about standards of behaviour and course etiquette in the old days, there is a lot of litter blowing around in this photo.

Bladders were obviously bigger back then, though, as there are no toilets in view.

The only tent that is advertising its wares (apart from the newspapers stand) is on the far right, a display of "old and rare golf clubs".

The wooden box (bottom right) has "pay here" on the side. It leads on to the course itself.

Access to the tented village, such as it was, was free.

■ Simpson's, just a few yards from the first tee, is the second oldest golf shop in the world. Robert Simpson (1862-1923) twice finished fourth at The Open, and his brother Jack won it in 1884. Born in Earlsferry, Bob (as he was known to all) came to be the professional at Dalhousie Golf Club in Carnoustie in 1883 and opened his shop almost immediately. As well as a renowned player, Robert was a skilled golf club maker – which was a craft of almost mystical artistry when clubs were made of wood. At one point he employed around 30 artisans in his club-making workshop. The clubs they produced are, to this day, regarded as among the finest ever made and they are renowned throughout the golfing world.

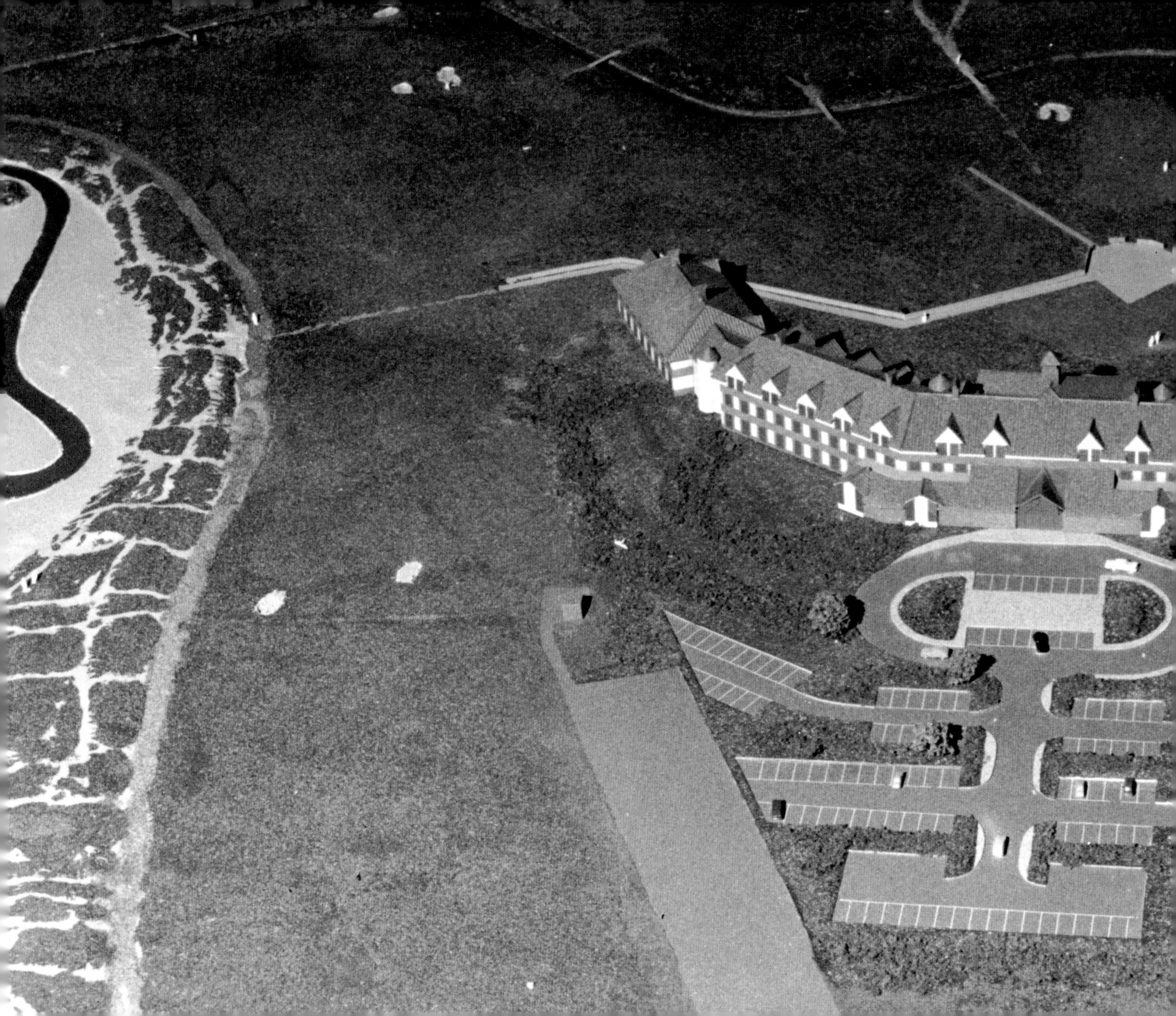

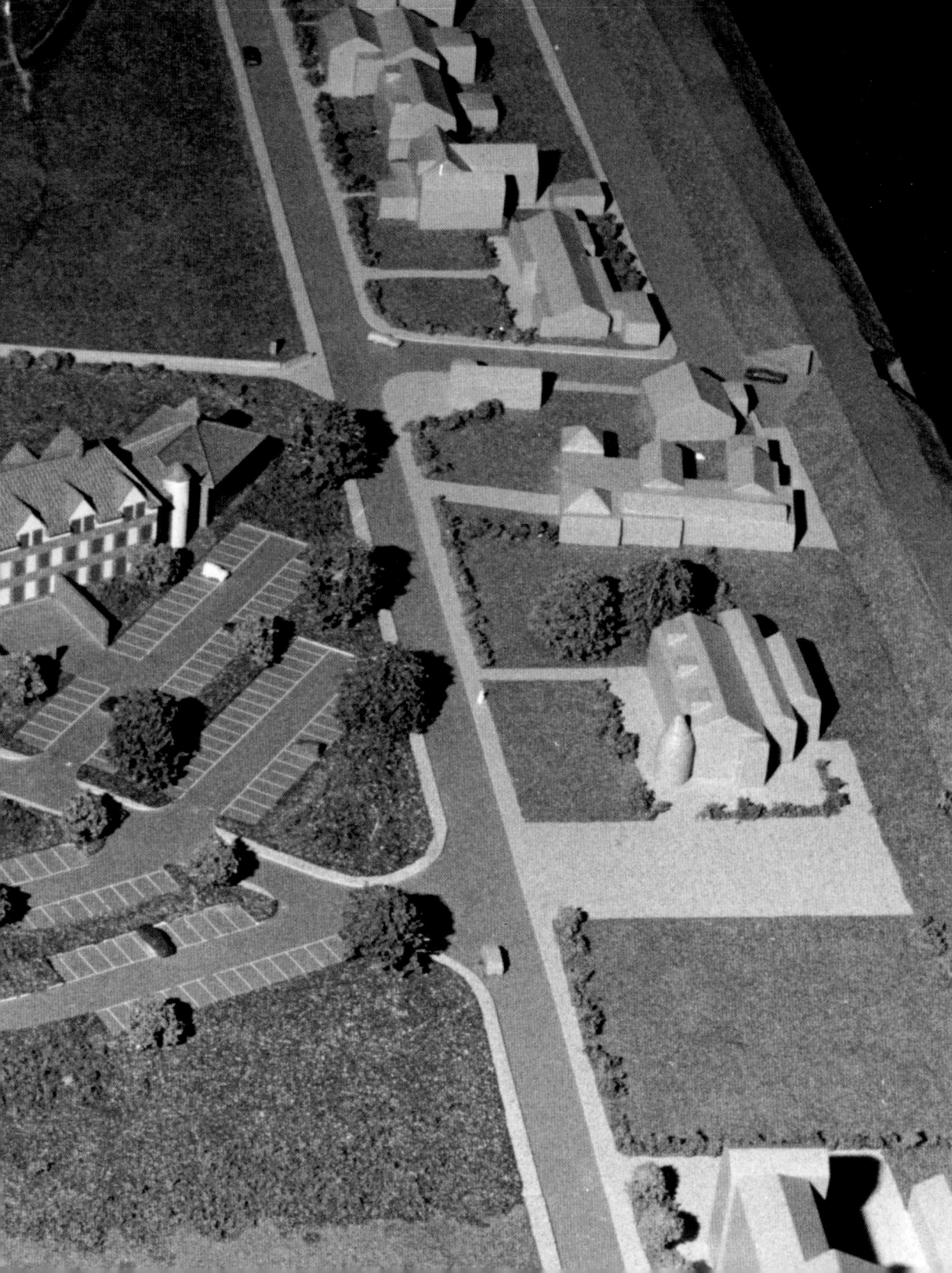

■ **Carnoustie didn't host an Open between 1975 and 1999. One of the reasons for this 24-year period without a tournament was the absence of a world-class hotel.**

Various plans had been advanced during those years without an Open.

This model, was displayed to residents of the town in 1988, showing how a proposed hotel might look.

The building, finished in 1999, just in time for The Open that year, ended up being a little different to this but there are also many similarities.

It was very welcome. The Open could return to town, and the Carnoustie course could take its place once more as the most exacting test of tournament golf anywhere in the British Isles.

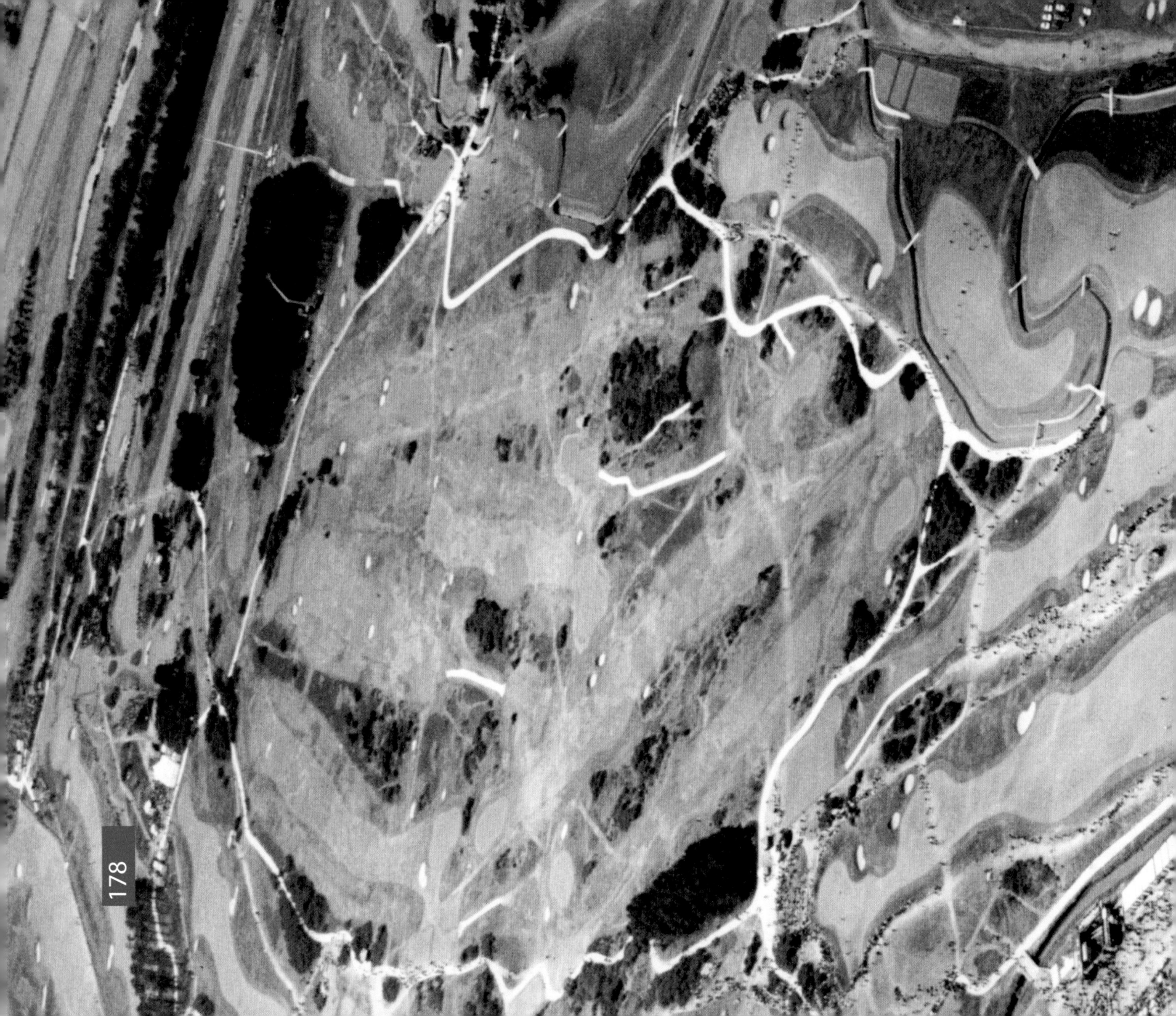

■ **You will have had to turn your book on its side to see this properly. This is Carnoustie links from the air, pictured during The Open of 1999 – famously won by Scotland's Paul Lawrie in a three-way play-off.**

The Championship Course, somewhat unusually, is laid out around the outer perimeter of another course, the Burnside (see the 1937 map on page 62). The back nine is a particularly stern test of golf. There are no less than five crosses of the snaking burn in the last two holes alone.

There is a saying in Carnoustie that speaks volumes for exactly what the course is. It goes: "Only good golfers enjoy to play here." it is a testament to the magnitude of the task that is faced.

■ Above and right: Another two shots of the 1953 Open. The big draw was the great Ben Hogan (see page 90). As can be seen here, Carnoustie's golf course starts and finishes almost within the town. The thoroughfare alongside the course, Links Parade, is a street much like any other in Carnoustie.

It has also been said that the course isn't the prettiest, or that the views from it aren't very memorable. Perhaps so, but then (as seen here) they have put some bunting up.

In any case if you go to Carnoustie to play golf, you won't have time to take in the views. The course will require all, absolutely all, of your concentration.

■ The scoreboard wasn't a continuously-updated piece of electronic whizzmagiggery as they are nowadays, although the staff did as well as they could under the circumstances. But it is apparent, given the attention the scores are attracting here, that this was an important part of the spectator experience (though they wouldn't have used a term like "spectator experience" in the 1950s!)

■ 1953. The first green.

184

■ Two further photos of the 1953 Open. No big grandstands in those days. Plainly visible on the dunes, however, are the coastal defences – lines of concrete tank traps and pill boxes – left over from the war. Delicate negotiations on the placement of these had taken place to make sure they impacted as little as possible on the links. Fighting off a Nazi invasion was one thing, interrupting the golf was quite another!

■ **The 1953 Open was a well-attended event. Indeed, the number of cars that came to town was a bit of a surprise. Car ownership wasn't very widespread in those austere times.**

An influx of so many private cars had never happened before at Carnoustie. Finding parking was a bit of a problem, with various hasty suggestions made for where, around the town, the overspill might be directed to.

The real problem became apparent after the tournament finished, however.

The course at Carnoustie is hemmed in by the Dundee to Aberdeen railway line, with only a few narrow access points (this is still a problem today). So the jams when cars were attempting to leave all at once lasted several hours, with some rather irate drivers sitting for a long time without progressing an inch.

Carnoustie vowed to get it right the next time The Open visited, though that wouldn't be for a further 15 years.

■ **Right: Among those attending the 1953 Open was a certain Mr F. Sinatra, pictured here in the tented village.**

Frank had left his wife at the time, Ava Gardner, shopping in Dundee while he had a day out watching Hogan.

The great crooner also took the opportunity to arrange a concert at Dundee's Caird Hall while he was in the area.

However, the 3,300-seat venue had only 600 at the first showing, and 1,189 for the 8.45pm second house.

The low attendances were attributed to the expensive ticket prices, which ranged from five shillings (25 pence in modern money) to 15 shillings (75p).

■ By the time the 1968 Open came to town, the game had become more commercialised, with vast grandstands. Though it must be said that, at that time, some of the stands (especially those further out on the course) were free to sit in.

The problem of car parking was hived off to fields on the outskirts of town.

■ The Barry Burn, a snaking hazard with a venomous bite.

■ **Above:** May 1967. The end is nigh for the old starter's box.
■ **Right:** A slightly light-damaged photo of The Open of 1968, showing a lot of thorny gorse bush to lose your ball, possibly yourself, in.

■ The 18th green at the 1975 Open. Note the difference in the surrounds from the earlier shots of tournaments at Carnoustie.

The 1960s

Tony Lema at the 1964 Open.

It was always Scotland's game

IT has been said that Scottish golf "re-emerged" on to the world stage in the 1960s. The Open regained its place as the most prestigious Major, and America (and her golfing enthusiasts) began to pay a great deal of attention to Scotland, and flocked to play here.

It is perhaps truer to say that the surrounding elements of the game in Scotland began to catch up with the rest of the world in the 1960s. Golf had, for several decades, flourished overseas – especially in the USA. It had massively risen in popularity and a lot of money had started swirling around.

Here in Scotland, those who followed the game were a little bemused to be rediscovered. They didn't know they'd been lost! The game's great traditions had remained the same, and very good players were still being produced.

It is incontrovertibly true, however, to say that a new level of professionalism was imported into Scotland in the '60s. Marketing of the game and knowledge of the potential benefits in the off-course industry woke us up. Again, a wee bit of a surprise, as we hadn't realised we'd been asleep.

Television helped make this transformation, as did easier and quicker intercontinental jet travel. Lessons in how to sell the game were also learned.

But what hadn't changed was the fact that the greatest golf courses in the world were still here – as they always had been.

That's why Scotland remains the home of golf.

Football, rugby, tennis and many other sports started in Britain, but the focus of attention for these other games – the best proponents, the greatest stadiums, the biggest money – are now elsewhere.

That can't happen to golf in the same way. Because nowhere else are there such courses as there are here.

You can design beautiful courses in foreign lands and call them great – and there are many very good courses around the world – but they aren't quite the same as a Scottish links. You can't take The Old Course to another country.

Please don't take this as a complaint or think us bitter. We in Scotland are grateful for the way the game has been developed. We admire the great players – and administrators – who took the game to such stratospheric levels.

But it was always Scotland's game.

■ **Opposite: Tony Lema winning the 1964 Open at St Andrews. This would be Tony's only Major. Two years later the talented American died, aged 32, along with his pregnant wife Betty, in a plane crash near Chicago.**

200

The Big Three

ALONG with the rest of the golfing world, Scotland was mesmerised by "The Big Three" in the 1960s.

Arnold Palmer, Gary Player and Jack Nicklaus were important forces of the game's rise in popularity.

And, of course, they came to Scotland. Each one of them has gone on record many times to talk about their love of the Scottish links game.

They can be paid the highest accolade that any man can have – all three are regarded as honorary Scotsmen. With their prodigious golfing talent they must surely have Scots blood in them somewhere!

There are some great 1960s photos of those golfing giants, in their formidable prime, in Scottish settings.

Hallowed be their names.

■ **Left: St Andrews 1960 – Arnie relaxes in the sun before teeing-off in his first ever Open.**

■ **Right: Arnie plays his way out of a bunker on his way to winning at Troon in 1962.**

■ The Big Three at ease and swapping jokes during practice for the 1966 Muirfield Open.

203

204

Arnie was the saviour

IF the Scottish golf "resurrection" had to have just one hero, it would be Arnold Palmer.

The Open, in the post-war era, clashed dates with the PGA Championship in the USA – which paid much more money – and the top American golfers stayed at home to take part in it. Who could blame them.

This meant that, in the opinion of the rest of the world, The Open wasn't really a major competition any more. How could it be when the top players didn't come to compete? By the late 1950s, this had become a real problem.

But, inspired by Bobby Jones's grand slam in 1930, and thinking he might match Ben Hogan's victory in 1953, Arnie came to play The Open at St Andrews in 1960. He had won The Masters and the US Open (as Hogan had done in 1953).

The world was agog to see if he could take a third major in a calendar year. The American golfing media, usually focused on their own tour, turned their eyes to Fife. And they liked what they saw.

St Andrews wasn't like a US circuit tournament. It had centuries of history, esoteric traditions, and more than a few quaint oddities. For instance, by the rules, Arnie – the world's best player – had to come through a 36-hole qualifying round. There was also a quite remarkable flood (see page 338).

It all made for great TV entertainment.

Arnie didn't win that tournament; he was runner-up to Australia's Kel Nagle. But for ever after The Open was indisputably returned to its position as a world-renowned tournament and a highlight of the golf year.

Arnie changed the course of history for golf in the UK. We will forever be grateful.

■ **The angle of this photo doesn't afford a view of the crowd Arnie is waving to. But rest assured the galleries welcomed him with massive enthusiasm. Crowds at the 1960 Open were double those of 1959.**

■ If there is one photo to illustrate the impact Arnie's 1960 appearance had, then this shot of the gallery following him must be it. St Andrews had never seen anything like this. It was obvious to even the most venerable old curmudgeons of golf – the game had changed for ever.

■ Arnie was big news everywhere he went, and was filmed from all angles. The cameraman in the photo on the left went to extraordinary lengths (with Arnie's permission of course) to get an unusual shot of the great man's swing. Golf on TV was big business.

210

- Left: Arnie – Open winner 1961.
- This page: Gary – Open winner 1968.

212

■ **The 1962 Open at Troon.**

Arnie just misses a putt on the 18th that would have given him an incredible 66 for his third round, played on the Friday morning.

He was five shots ahead at this point.

Arnie then shot a 69 in the afternoon and took the championship by six strokes. It was a superb display of golf by "The King".

The crowd paid 10 shillings (50p) each to see the two rounds on that final day.

The 2022 equivalent of 10 shillings is about £11.15.

■ The charismatic Arnie with the 1962 Open trophy.

■ Jack would outstrip them all. He is seen here as barely more than a kid in 1964, and (opposite) about to play Doug Sanders in the 1970 Open play-off. You can tell from their expressions who is going to win!

218

■ Left: Gene Sarazen, who was 58 at the time this photo was taken at the 1960 Open. He had been a star of golf since the 1920s.

He was, by this point, a revered and respected link with the past.

Gene had been a rival and contemporary of Bobby Jones and Walter Hagen.

■ Right: Jock Hutchison at St Andrews in 1960.

He is significant on both sides of the Atlantic for different reasons surrounding the same Open.

Jock remains, to this day, the last St Andrews-born (1884) man to win an Open Championship. He won in 1921.

Having moved to the US to pursue his golf career, he is remembered there as the first American to win The Open, having become a naturalised US citizen in 1920.

■ A fascinated gallery watches five-time Open winner Peter Thomson at St Andrews in 1960.

221

■ Australian Kel Nagle drops the Open-winning putt at St Andrews 1960.

224

■ **April 7th, 1963. Harry Weetman and Eric Brown putt on the 6th green at Carnoustie.**

The English and Scottish pros are seen here battling out a £100 challenge match – the winner taking £75, loser £25.

After a slow start, on a bitterly cold day, Brown won by a single hole.

Such exhibition matches were fairly common in the years after the war, and would often attract a good following.

In those days, with very little golf shown on TV, it was often the only chance spectators got to see professional golf played under competitive conditions.

The equivalent of £100 in 1963 would be about £2,200 in 2022.

■ This page and opposite: Sam Snead at practice during The Open Championship, Troon 1962. Although aged 49 at this point, Sam had been one of golf's biggest stars from the mid-1930s, and one of its great innovators. He pioneered "croquet-style" putting – standing facing the hole, one foot on either side of the ball – until it was banned by the USGA in 1968.

■ **Muirfield 1966.** This was Jack Nicklaus's fifth Open. He had been third in 1963, and second in 1964. By this point, it was the only major he hadn't won. He arrived in East Lothian determined to put that right.

■ **And what a thriller it was. Muirfield was set up with narrow fairways and knee-high rough but Jack – aided by his customary long, straight tee shots – battled through the back nine on the final day, nip and tuck with Doug Sanders and Dave Thomas. The lead changed hands several times but Jack won by a single stroke to complete his first career slam.**

■ **Jack again at Muirfield 1966.**

231

232

■ To the winner the spoils.
　Muirfield 1966 again, and Jack has just recorded his winning score in the caravan behind, and is greeted by his wife Barbara.
　Then (right) he is presented with the Claret Jug in front of the clubhouse.

　In early 2022 it was announced that Jack was to receive the highest honour that St Andrews can give: freedom of the town.
　It isn't often that anyone is granted this. It is a measure of character as well as sporting prowess.
　There has rarely been a more popular announcement in the town.

■ The course at Carnoustie, looking down the 17th fairway, set up for The Open of 1968.

■ Two rather distant shots of the starter's box at Carnoustie in 1966. The pic on the left looks east across the Barry Burn. Heaven help you if your ball lands in there! The photo above is looking westward, with the Championship Course behind the starter's box on the left of the shot. This photo was taken from the Bruce Hotel, the grand old building where so many of the game's stars lodged when playing at Carnoustie.

■ John Panton plays an approach to the 18th green during Open Qualifying at Monifieth in 1968. The tournament was at Carnoustie that year, just a few miles up the coast. Monifieth Medal gets less publicity than neighbours St Andrews or Carnoustie and is often described as an "underrated" course – except by those finding themselves in the rough on the tricky 4th, buffeted by a snell North Sea wind.

■ **A hazard that isn't mentioned in many golf brochures.**

A huge jet plane roaring over Troon Golf Course on its way to Prestwick Airport.

This is the 7th green, in 1969.

AS we celebrate the 150th Open, this photo looks back to the Centenary Open of 1960.

That year celebrated 100 years since the first Open, but was the 89th tournament, due to the world wars.

This photo of the R&A Centenary Open Dinner shows the top table. From left, 1923 Open champion Arthur Havers, the R&A's Thomas Harvey (partially hidden behind trophy), three-time open champion Henry Cotton, past R&A captain Colonel John Inglis, 1920 Open champion George Duncan, captain of the R&A Henry Turcan, and 1932 Open champion Gene Sarazen.

Also present at that historic Centenary Dinner were past champions Willie Auchterlonie, Jock Hutchison, Peter Thomson, Fred Daly, Dick Burton, Gary Player, Alf Padgham and Max Faulkner. And future champion Arnold Palmer.

It was a gathering of golf royalty!

The Open trophy – the Claret Jug – is placed centrally on the table. It has been presented to the year's champion golfer since 1872. A new trophy was required that year as Young Tom Morris had won the original Challenge Belt outright after his third triumph in a row.

The original Claret Jug remains in the R&A clubhouse. The trophy presented and kept by the champion is a replica.

■ **History and even more history.** In 1960, during the Centenary Dinner seen on the previous page, the reigning champion Gary Player, then aged 24, met Willie Auchterlonie who was at that time the oldest living former Open champion. Willie was 88 at this point. He had won the 1893 Open at Prestwick, at the age of 21. His purse was £30. Willie, who died in 1963 aged 90, was quite a character, a story-teller, and had a great knowledge of the game. He loved to talk and laugh, as the series of photos on the right (also from 1960) show.

Laurie Ayton Jnr at the 1960 Open.

He had been paired with another Scots pro, Eric Brown. They look almost alone and un-noticed on the course.

The gent behind, with the chalk-marked scores on a board he is carrying, gives a stark, and quite endearing, contrast to modern televised tournament play.

Nowadays, every digital graphic and gizmo is displayed beside each player's name, and every shot they play is tracked by the TV cameras.

Back then, media attention was a little less intrusive.

The 1970s

THE 1970s was a momentous time for golf. In truth, American players dominated the decade to a degree that hadn't been achieved before by any one country in the modern era, and has never happened again since.

Of the 40 majors played, 1970 to 1979, only Gary Player (4 wins), Tony Jacklin (2) and Seve Ballesteros (1) interrupted the flow of US victories.

The top-ranked Americans were superstars – big news wherever they played and, often (of course) they played in Scotland. Six of the 10 Opens held in the 1970s were played on Scottish links.

Off the course, world golf completed its transition from being a great sport to also being a great sporting industry. It has carried on growing in every decade since.

A lot of clever businesspeople saw opportunities and developed them. They made big investments and (mostly) got big returns.

Golf tourism was born in that decade. Golf equipment sales rocketed. The value of endorsements, advertising and marketing hit stratospheric heights.

But still it is a game that has its roots, and therefore largely owes its existence, to a handful of scrubby, low-lying patches of land scattered around the Scottish coasts.

■ **Right: A quiet and peaceful St Andrews in 1978. This photo was taken in May of that year, before preparations for the forthcoming Open had really begun.**

If you speak to any older resident of the Fife town they will tell you that each time, over the decades, that The Open came back to the Old Course everything got bigger, busier, brasher, noisier, and more expensive.

249

■ **There is a special reception given to former Open champions when they return to St Andrews.**

These great players are often unashamedly emotional as they cross the Swilcan Bridge and make their way up the 18th fairway, with every spectator in the gallery rising to afford them a standing ovation.

It is one of the great impromptu traditions of the Old Course. A measure of admiration and affection that goes far beyond any monetary measure of value.

This is Bobby Locke (left) impeccable in shirt and tie, as always, on the bridge in 1970. The fourth of his Open triumphs was won at St Andrews in 1957.

■ **Right: Jack Nicklaus adds his name to the list of St Andrews Open winners in 1970. Eight years later he would join an even shorter list – those who have won two Opens at St Andrews.**

252

■ **The Open at Troon 1973. Tom Weiskopf anxiously watches his putt on the first green. It is often possible for the top players to get a birdie on this par 4. The town is visible in the background, across the bay.**

254

■ **Practice day at Troon, 1973. Above: Jack Nicklaus has lost his ball in the long rough. They should have asked the dog in the background to help sniff it out!**
■ **Left: SuperMex Lee Trevino. The hugely popular Texan was going for his third Open in a row.**

■ The 1973 champion golfer Tom Weiskopf. It was the American's only major, and a wire-to-wire victory (a fairly rare occurrence for The Open). The sunny weather at the start of the tournament had given way to a downpour by the time the presentations were made. It was so wet that water got into the photographer's camera, damaging the film.

■ Gene Sarazen was presented with a bottle of Champagne to mark his hole-in-one at the 8th (Postage Stamp). Gene was aged 71 at the time, and this also marked 50 years since his first appearance at Troon for the 1923 Open. Gene, who died in 1999, was one of only five players to win a career slam. This presentation, however, appears to have taken place out of sight around the side of a tent!

258

■ **Right: Gary Player and Tom Weiskopf with Gary's renowned caddie Alfred "Rabbit" Dyer at The Open in Carnoustie in 1975.**
Rabbit, always ready with a joke or a quip, was almost as famous as Player himself!

■ **Left: Arnie with wife Winnie at that 1975 Open.**
Arnie was nearly 46 by this point and hadn't won a Major for 11 years. But he was still a superstar eagerly sought out by autograph hunters.

■ Slowly, players' families became more visible in the game during the 1970s. Aussie Jack Newton lost a dramatic play-off by a single stroke to Tom Watson in the 1975 Open at Carnoustie. At the trophy ceremony (on a dreich Angus afternoon) both men were joined by their wives – Jackie Newton (above) and Linda Watson (on opposite page). This was the last 18-hole Open play-off. Tied winning scores were settled by four-hole shoot-outs from 1985 onwards (although none were needed until 1989).

Four champions at Carnoustie in 1975. These men would amass an impressive 10 Claret Jugs between them.

■ Left: Three greats get in a practice round.
From left: Bobby Locke (then aged 57) a four-time winner of The Open; Max Faulkner (aged 58), the champion golfer of 1951; and comparative youngster Kel Nagle (54), the champion of 1960.
When the tournament started, Bobby showed a flash of his old magic at the first, holing his second shot for a magnificent eagle two.

■ Right: Tom Watson holds the trophy aloft at the end of the tournament. This was the first of his five Open victories, and first of his eight Majors.

■ **A gathering of younger stars at the Carnoustie Open, 1975.**

Left: David Chillas drives with Ronnie Shade and Jim Farmer looking on.

David enjoyed considerable success on the European tour before becoming a successful businessman.

Ronnie's nickname was RDBM (right down the bloody middle). He won the Scottish Amateur five consecutive times.

Jim Farmer went on to be a highly respected player, coach and administrator and was honorary pro at the R&A.

Right, a 21-year-old Sam Torrance. Sam topped them all, playing in eight Ryder cups (winning four) and captaining the team in 2002.

Australian Ian Stanley is on the left of the pic.

Not all of these men are still with us, but they were – and still are – revered golfing names.

■ The Open at Turnberry in 1977. The champion golfer of 1969, Tony Jacklin, chats with Henry Cotton.
■ Right: a 20-year-old Seve Ballesteros poses for the cameras.

Four more photos from Turnberry 1977.
- Left: Arnie in the burn at the third.
- Above: Aussie David Graham.
- Right: the unique fashion sense of Brian Barnes.
- Far right: Big Jack drives.

270

■ **A calm practice day, just before the St Andrews Open of 1978 got under way.**

There remained an innocent, natural charm and quirkiness about the Old Course and the surrounding links in the 1970s. But this was one of the things that TV audiences around the world loved.

And it wasn't only TV; the crowd record for an Open was broken on just the third day of this tournament.

There were huge queues as it was largely pay-at-the-gate, so no one had known how many people were going to turn up. The vast crowds almost swamped the unprepared staff at the pay booths.

■ My apologies, you'll have had to turn your book on its side again. Everyone got the fairytale ending they'd come to see.

Jack Nicklaus, the world's favourite golfer, won that 1978 Open, the second time he had triumphed in the tournament on the Old Course, and his third (and last) Claret Jug overall.

This, too, was a marketing person's dream. A victory to make everyone happy, that made them fall in love with the game just a little bit more . . . and that made them more likely to put their hands in their pockets in future, hoping to again see a cast of dashing heroes play out delightful dramas.

■ The huge 1978 crowds pour out their love and admiration for The Golden Bear.

The Walker Cup – at last!

BY 1971 The Walker Cup was 51 years old. It had been played for 22 times. GB&I had won it once, in 1938.

There had been some forgettable scorelines in that time, including two 11-1 drubbings in 1928 and 1961, several 10-2s, and a 10½-1½.

This couldn't go on.

So the tournament was brought back to the Old Course for the first time in 16 years. It was the 50th anniversary of the first unofficial match-up in 1921 at Royal Liverpool.

The USA team was formidable, and included future professional Major winners Lanny Wadkins and Tom Kite.

But captain Mike Bonallack was never an easily-daunted sort of chap and the Brits set about the task with gusto. They won the opening morning's foursomes 4-0.

The Americans fought back in the afternoon singles to lead 6½-5½ at close of play on the Thursday.

The next day, GB&I found themselves 9-7 down after the foursomes but stormed back to take six of the eight afternoon singles for an overall 13-11 win.

All who watched the play said the atmosphere among the galleries over those two days (and especially during the second day's singles games) was superb – loud and enthusiastic. But, above all, they remained polite, respectful and sporting at all times.

Standards of behaviour during team golf tournaments have grown to be somewhat more partisan and rather less sporting in recent years.

If the playing of the game itself, and the industry surrounding it, have changed over the years as commercialism grew and grew, then the watching of the game has also changed.

And not for the better.

Here in Scotland, spectators would always take pride in their good-natured, fair, and respectful behaviour when watching the game.

Or, at least, they used to.

■ **Right: The Great Britain & Ireland Walker Cup team of 1971. Back, from left; Charlie Green (Scotland), Hugh Stuart (Scotland), Michael Bonallack (England), Rodney Foster (England), George Macgregor (Scotland). Front: David Marsh (England), Warren Humphreys (England), Geoff Marks (England), Scott Macdonald (Scotland), Roddy Carr (Republic of Ireland).**

St Andrews, seen from above

THE Grand Old Lady stretches out from the town, ribbon-like across the triangle-shaped peninsula that is St Andrews Links.

This is not hilly terrain. In parts it is just a few feet above the high-tide mark – that's what "links" are, after all, low coastal areas with very few trees. From ground level it can look flat and deceptively featureless – the devilish folds and traps that lie in wait aren't apparent.

These bird's eye-view photos don't really reveal those hazards either – in fact the subtle dangers aren't fully appreciated until you are standing over your ball wondering what can possibly save you now. Three wood? Sand wedge? Divine intervention?

What these photos do show well is the extent of the course, and its position in relation to the town.

They also illustrate how exposed and open the links are to the sometimes furious winds that can hurtle in from the North Sea and make Scottish links golf such a challenge.

There was only one course to start with, but St Andrews links is now home to seven golf courses.

■ **This photo was taken during the 1957 Open, from the north, looking into the town.**

280

■ **1957 again. The 86th Open, looking over the West Sands, roughly towards the south.**

The first tee at the clubhouse are on the left, with the Swilken Burn looping over the 1st and 18th fairways on the right of the photo.

The tented village, such as it was in those days, is in the foreground and the northern stretches of the town in the background.

■ **The long West Sands, with the Old and New courses are shown in this 1957 photo. The railway curves away across the Fife countryside.**

Fife is a peninsula, bounded by the North Sea to the east, the Forth (to the south) and Tay (to the north) estuaries. At the western edge of the county is the natural barrier of the Ochil Hills.

This means Fife is, almost, cut off from the rest of Scotland – and was even more so before the building of the Forth rail (1889) and road (1964) bridges, and the Tay rail (1883) and road (1966) bridges.

This gives it a slightly different character to the rest of the country, which Fifers are often proud of (if they mention it) but may resent (if anyone else mentions it).

The East Neuk (neuk, pronounced nook, is an old Scots word for "corner") where St Andrews lies is a peninsula of the Fife peninsula. It is, if anything, the quietest part of a quiet county.

The East Neuk is, however, truly beautiful with several picturesque old fishing villages. It has the highest concentration of holiday homes in Scotland and is well worth a visit.

Tentsmuir Forest, with the Firth of Tay almost visible, is at the top of this photo. This is a fairly recent addition to the landscape, being planted in the 1920s, and is made up mostly of pine trees.

It was moorland and dunes before that.

284

■ Left: 1957 again, a view of the Old Course, bounded by the Eden River to the left and above, and North Sea on the right.

St Andrews Links holds the distinction of being a peninsula of the East Neuk, which is a peninsula of Fife, which is a peninsula of Scotland.

■ Right: the rail line that served the town closed in 1969, along with the railway station.

There have been many calls to have a line opened again. The StARLink (St Andrews Rail Link) campaign continues the fight.

And they are right, St Andrews should be on the UK rail network

■ This 1978 photo gives a slightly better impression of the proximity of the St Andrews and Carnoustie courses. They are just short of 11 miles apart, as the crow flies, across the Tay Estuary. It is a 25-mile journey by road, although needed a ferry crossing on a "Fifie" before the Tay Road Bridge was built. Two of the world's greatest golf courses within 11 miles might seem odd to anyone outside Scotland, but has always been merely "the way it is" to those living in the area. The novelty wore off long ago.

■ 1978 again. The tented village and car-parking areas have grown markedly from the 1957 versions (though still nothing like the extent of the huge complex at the 2022 Open). The loss of the rail connection will, of course, have increased the amount of road transport.

The changes to the game over the decades, and how the game looks, are illustrated and explored to a larger degree in a chapter starting on page 298.

■ Another two 1955 views.

■ The 5th and 13th green. One of the largest putting surfaces in world golf.

■ The town and course in 1955 (left) and 1978 (above). The town has grown significantly. Its population is now around 18,500, up from 14,209 in the 2001 National Census, and 11,000 in the 1951 census. House prices in the area are, by Scottish standards, high. St Andrews is seen as a very desirable place to live.

■ Another 1955 (left) and 1978 (above) Open Championships comparison, from opposing angles. There are differences, but also constants.

■ A long shot of the West Sands, with the Old Course off to the right. This shows, mainly, the New and Jubilee courses and the West Sands parking area. Be careful of the mounds and hollows where you park if a wet day is expected, you wouldn't be the first to return to find your car in a large puddle. It is another photo from 1978.

The Changing Face of the Game

■ **November 1967. The old Carnoustie starter's box in the foreground in the last few days before being replaced by the angular new clubhouse behind. That clubhouse was replaced, in turn, in the late 1990s with the construction of the current Carnoustie Golf Hotel building.**

NOTHING stays the same. Golf has had to move with the times, and the times are ever changing.

This book's aim has been to show the game, and the places where it is played, in Scotland over the course of the past 60 or 70 years.

There are a few older photos, but in the main this is how golf might be remembered by a long-lived enthusiast. And that long-lived golfer has seen an awful lot of changes.

The game has changed, the way tournaments are staged has changed. Equipment has changed.

People have changed too. The way they want to

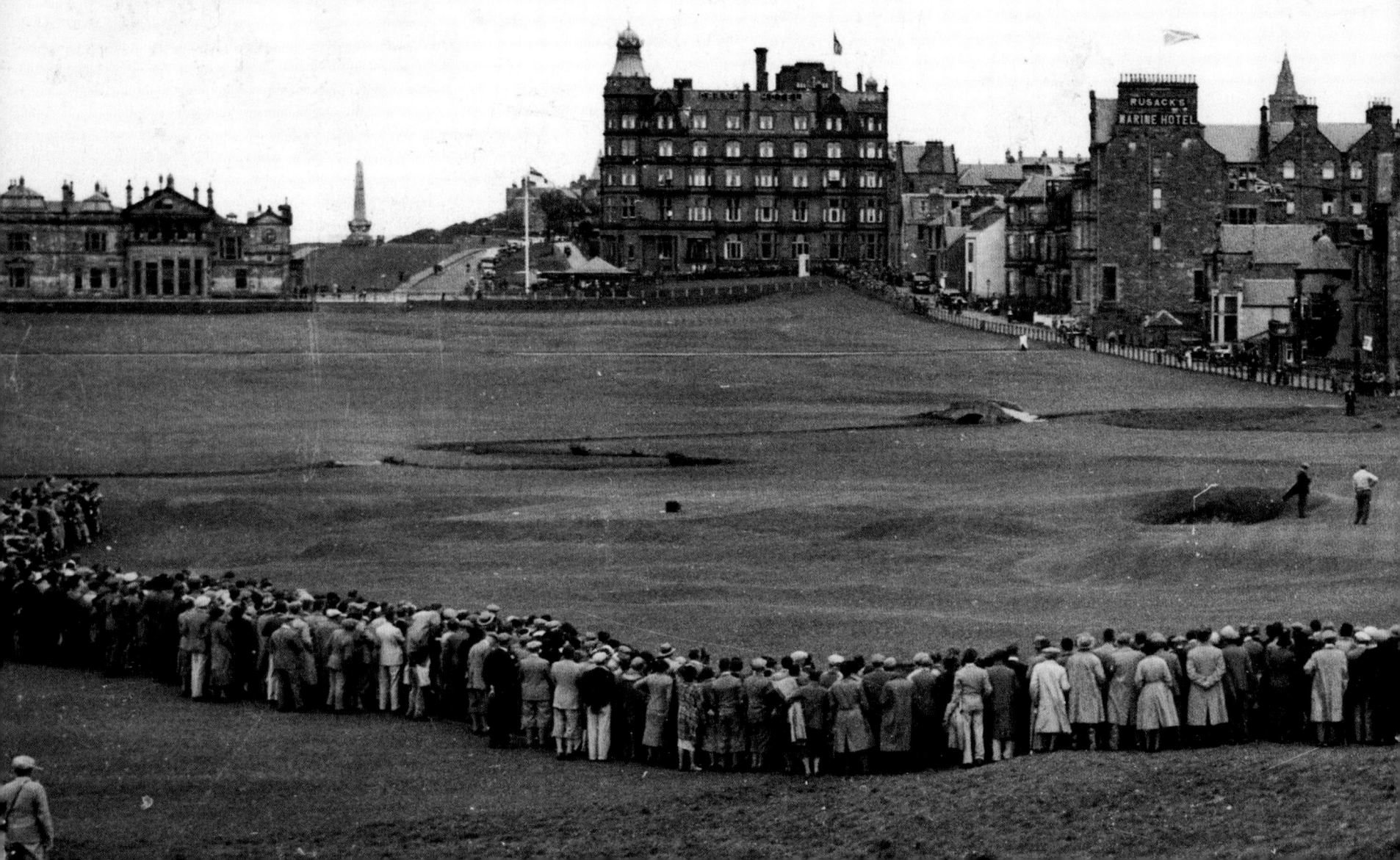

watch the game and their behaviour while doing so has changed.

The big question is: was it better in the old days?

Or have the innovations, new-found comforts, and slick presentation improved the experience of what it is to be a golf lover?

Only you can judge your opinion on that.

This book has merely presented you with some points and views to consider.

■ **This photo shows Sam Snead on his way to winning The Open at St Andrews in 1946.**

■ The pace of change has greatly increased. The photo above is the Walker Cup at St Andrews in 1947. It is very like the 1946 pic on the previous page. On the right is the final day's play at The Open 1970. Not a lot is different over the span of 23 years. There is a modest grandstand in front of the Hamilton Grand in 1970, and (out of shot to the left) another grandstand bordering the first fairway. But the potential of the game

hadn't yet been fully realised. After 1970, The Open didn't return to Fife until 1978, the eight-year gap being an unusually long time between St Andrews Opens. But when it did come back it was completely different proposition. It was a world event. And it has continued to evolve at great pace, as anyone who has been a guest at modern corporate hospitality, or even wandered through the tented village, will know. It's a different planet.

304

■ Stampede! Police race to create a cordon to hold the crowd. This was the 1984 Open, with Seve Ballesteros about to win his second Claret Jug.
   You didn't see scenes like these at Opens of yesteryear.

■ **Another photo of the 1984 Open at St Andrews. Tom Watson emerges from the melee to make his way up the 18th fairway.**

If you are of a sufficient age to remember, cast your mind back to the way tournaments were in the 1950s (or leaf back through the pages of this book). One of the biggest differences is the level of noise.

Modern tournaments are very loud. Tournaments of old had a smattering of applause amid an otherwise quiet atmosphere. Modern tournaments have roars.

It is perhaps too simplistic to say that the older, more civilised ways were better, or more dignified. Many players enjoy applause. They appreciate being appreciated.

And it is a fine thing to behold a revered champion marching up the 18th on the final day of a tournament being greeted with a heartfelt standing ovation from the packed galleries.

■ **Even the most ardent traditionalist would have to admit this is an impressive sight, and a ringing endorsement for the popularity of golf.**

■ The St Andrews Opens of 1955 (above) and 1961 (right). These were altogether quieter affairs. The winners were Peter Thomson (1955) and Kel Nagle (1960).

■ 1960. Greenkeepers Hugh Burnett, David Laing and Bert Moffat put the final touches to the bunker guarding the 17th green at St Andrews. The fine points of course preparation were done by hand. Greenkeepers were skilled and knowledgeable men (as they still are) who knew every blade of grass and grain of sand on their courses. Many a wily golfer has sought the advice of a greenkeeper on how a course plays.

■ The Walker Cup scoreboard 1955, updated by signwriters with pots of paint, brushes, and a steady hand.

314

■ This was one of the main reasons that everything changed. Television revenues poured in as broadcasters were given ever more access to screen extensive footage of the big tournaments. This photo shows Henry Cotton playing an exhibition at The Old Course in 1961, with cameras and sound equipment all around him.

■ The outside and (opposite page) inside of the new (in 1967) clubhouse at Carnoustie heralded changes in the way watching golf at the course was experienced. The 1968 Open was the first time multiple grandstands were erected at the Carnoustie course.

318

■ **Above:** the Old Course Hotel was originally the British Transport Hotel, and opened in 1968. This photo is from 1983, showing Frank Sherridan (left), owner of the hotel at that point, with Keith Mackie (golf director) in what would become the new lounge, an addition to the original building. The hotel sits on seaside links land so its foundations required innovative underground floats to give stability on the deep-seated, ever-shifting sands.
■ **Left:** a 1968 view of the new hotel from the second tee of the Old Course.

■ Corporate hospitality at The Old Course Hotel in 1984 – golf in beautiful surroundings, a sumptuous meal, fine wines, a dram of whisky afterwards. And no chance of being blown into an ankle-deep puddle by a malevolent gust of rain-laden wind from the North Sea. You can see why hospitality became popular!

■ **The Open 1970.** The fact that a photographer was moved to take a shot of a grandstand being built is significant. They were strange, alien beasts, never before seen in these parts. They were a source of wonder, a news item worthy of reporting in the local papers.

■ Turnberry 1977. A Japanese visitor with a portable television – which was very impressive tech for the mid-1970s. Today, of course, a good number of spectators at any golf tournament aren't watching what is going on around them, they have their heads bowed looking at footage on their mobile phones.

■ **By the time of the St Andrews Open of 1984, they were even putting up grandstands beside the Road Hole. This was a wee bit of a shock to traditionalists, who had always regarded this area as one of the 17th's hazards – not quite an official part of the course, perhaps, but "in play" if you'd hit a particularly wayward second shot.**

326

■ Crowd control at the 16th tee during the Walker Cup, 1971. The men with long sticks kept order. They held these sticks at waist height, forming a linked barrier – sure in the knowledge that no one would be so uncouth that they might push past.

■ **There has always been a thriving golf equipment market.**

Clubs, bags, balls and clothing, of course, but also a large number of sometimes innovative, sometimes odd, "gadgets".

On the left is "Electro Golf" which promised the user could play any course in the world.

They hit a shot at a screen which had the holes of a course projected on to it by the little box beside the balls in this photo.

The impact was measured for distance and accuracy . . . and a vague approximation made of where your ball might have ended up.

Modern simulators have become quite sophisticated, but this was very advanced, and very novel, for 1964.

On the right is a ball collector first seen in Scotland in 1955, which was a very good idea, and caught on with golfers. Its great-grandchildren are still in use today.

■ **If there weren't golf gadgets to spend our money on we'd just waste it on rubbish!**

Over the years, many an idea to ease the burden of carrying clubs (and players) round the course has been marketed.

The "Electrical Caddy Car" on this page was marketed as early as 1956, and ran off a full-size car battery – which would probably have been heavier than the club and bags.

The electric golf cart on the right is from 1959 and shows Gleneagles pro Jack McLean with a man named as Mr Francis Brown, "the Hawaiian pineapple king", who was a guest at Gleneagles Hotel.

Jack was pro at the King's Course, a highly respected figure in the Scottish game who died at the tragically young age of 50 in 1961.

He won three Scottish Amateur Championships in a row in the 1930s and was leading amateur at The Opens of 1933 and 1934.

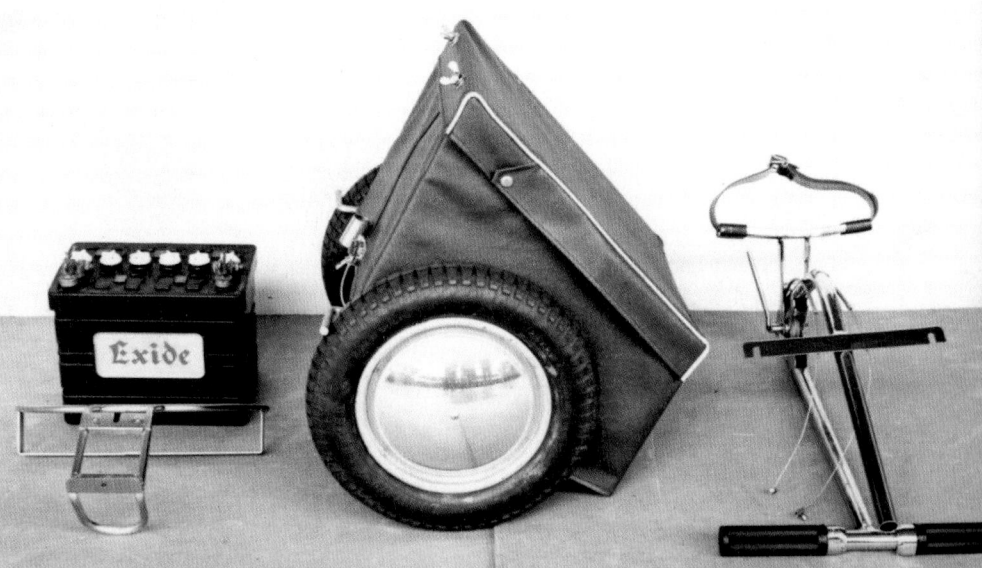

331

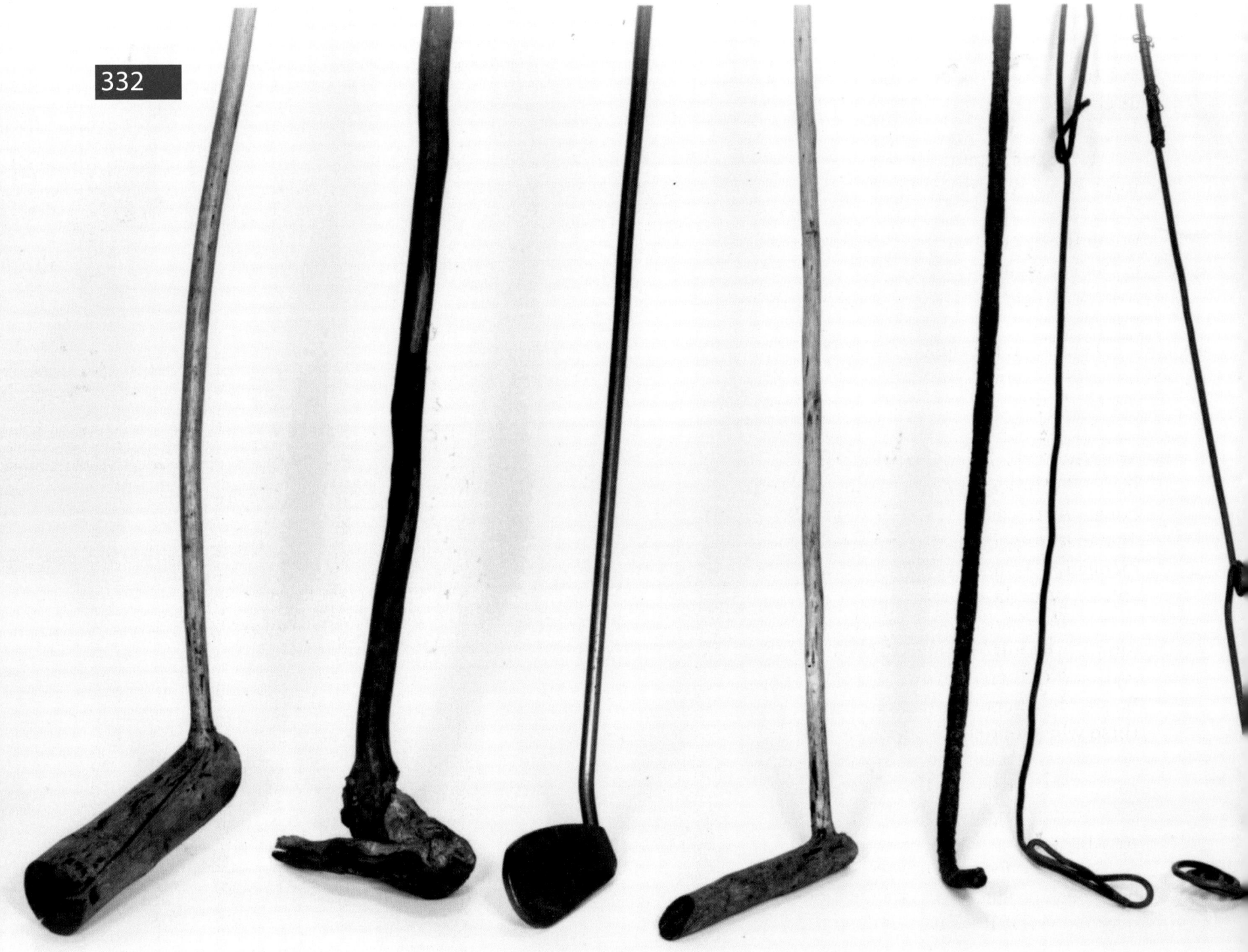

■ **Club design has changed as much as anything in golf.**

The primitive examples on the left are from the early years of the game.

A "special" set of clubs – a new make, revolutionary design or material, or clubs promoted with the name of a player (buy my clubs, play like me) – has always been big business.

The set on the right were crafted in the late 1980s from the propellers of the QE2, the world's most famous passenger liner.

The QE2 clubs, made by Swilken of St Andrews, had quite a tale behind them. The process of purchasing, melting down and re-casting two 32-tonne, 19ft-diameter propellers, made of aluminium manganese bronze, was never going to be entirely straightforward!

They are shown here on sale at Simpson's Golf Shop in Carnoustie in April 1990. Swilken's Dave McNicoll is flanked by Brenda Goddard and Jenny Birse who worked at Simpson's.

The clubs went down very well with customers, especially those in the Far East, and examples of QE2s still crop up for sale today.

And countless other "special" clubs have been produced around the world over the years. It's a part of the game.

In Scotland, golf is an all-weather sport

ST ANDREWS is 150 miles further north than Toronto, and on roughly the same latitude as Moscow. But Scotland doesn't suffer the same ice-bound winters as these places.

The (relatively) benign weather is due to the Gulf Stream keeping the surrounding seas warm. The accompanying North Atlantic winds pick up hot southern air and carry it towards the low air pressure areas around Iceland.

This clash of humid air and cold air keeps the temperature above freezing (usually) but results in a succession of mini-depressions being pushed over Scotland. They bring lots of cloud and lots of rain. This usually rolls in from the west.

When the wind blows from the other direction, the North Sea produces banks of chewy-thick fog (that we call haar) in coastal areas.

Yes, the weather can make golf a tad difficult in Scotland.

And this is part of the attraction. Tales are often told of golf tourists from the Americas or Far East who are disappointed to play one of our great courses on a nice day.

They want to wrestle Car-nasty in a snell wind, or hack their way round a dreich Old Course suffering a sullen chill – because those are the fabled "real tests of golf". The days they have read about or seen on TV. The days when golf is a battle.

Drives are blown wildly off course, approach shots hold up or fly too far – but you can't see where the ball went anyway for the hailstones hurtling across the fairway like machine-gun fire.

That is Scottish links golf with its teeth bared.

336

■ **Living on an island.**

The morning after a night of persistent rain in 1988, the clubhouse at Carnoustie is almost surrounded by a huge puddle.

This somewhat contradicts the oft-repeated notion that links land, usually a thin layer of topsoil over sand, drains easily and quickly.

■ Scotland has what meteorologists term a "temperate" climate, so extreme weather events are rare. A cloudburst in which a month's rain falls in a few hours should happen only two or three times every century in any one place. It would be incredibly unlucky for such a thing to happen during a major golf tournament. But that is exactly what befell the St Andrews Open of 1960. Unprecedented rainfall on the Friday afternoon forced the final round to be held over until the Saturday – the first time this had happened to an Open in more than 50 years. The following eight pages are scenes from that incredibly wet day, which is still talked about in Fife.

340

■ The heavens opened, dumping so much water on the course so quickly that there was nowhere for it to go. It sat in puddles that were, in places, several feet deep.

■ There was only one thing to do – call in the Fire Brigade, who were used to pumping water (although usually pouring it out rather than gathering it in).

■ Play resumed the following day. Joe Carr and Guy Wolstenholme stroll by the puddles on the second fairway. The two were the leading amateurs in the tournament.

■ Carnoustie again, 1966 on this page and 1988 opposite. Water features are found on many golf courses around the world – which is fine when they behave, but very troublesome when they do not. These are two examples of the Barry Burn bursting its banks and flooding Carnoustie's fairways after torrential rainfall.

■ Deep snow covers Scotland's mountains for months at a time in winter, but the salty seaside air will usually thaw out links land quickly – even when areas just a mile or so inland retain knee-deep drifts.

But this snowfall, of January 1960, took a long time to shift.

The snow cover gives the Old Course a very unusual look. Photos like this are rare.

350

■ **The winter of 1963 was the worst that Scotland suffered in the entire 20th Century. Snow fell, then was frozen in place by several weeks of sub-zero temperatures.**

This meant the Old Course was under a blanket of ice for several months, a highly unusual occurrence.

Before the course was to reopen, on April 1st, it was given a good brush up in preparation for hosting the British Amateur in June – won by Michael Lunt.

He would go on to be captain of the R&A in 2007, although he sadly died during his captaincy.

■ May 29th, 1975. St Andrews hosts The Walker Cup (US 15½, UK&I 8½). It is two days short of June. But see the buttoned-up coats, count the brollies, take note of the stout footwear. It can be bitterly cold on a St Andrews summer day!

353

■ **Perhaps most amazingly of all, despite the horrors the elements can throw the Scottish public stoically comes out to watch golf.**

■ Left: The crowds who braved thunder, lightning and pelting rain to follow the final of the Scottish Amateur at the Old Course in July 1971.

It was worth watching.

Sandy Stephen, a 17-year-old schoolboy from nearby Buckhaven defeated veteran, and defending champion Charlie Green 3 and 2.

The game should have finished on Saturday, but there were so many puddles it was decided to hold over the last couple of holes until the Sunday.

But this wasn't a straightforward affair at St Andrews. Sunday play, in those days, wasn't normally permitted. An application for such a thing had to be made months in advance to the Town Council – which hadn't been done.

Luckily, the Provost at the time, David Niven, gave the go-ahead.

■ **Right: Peter Oosterhuis on his way to tying for 7th place at The Open at Carnoustie 1975. The forest of umbrellas in the background tell you what sort of day it was!**

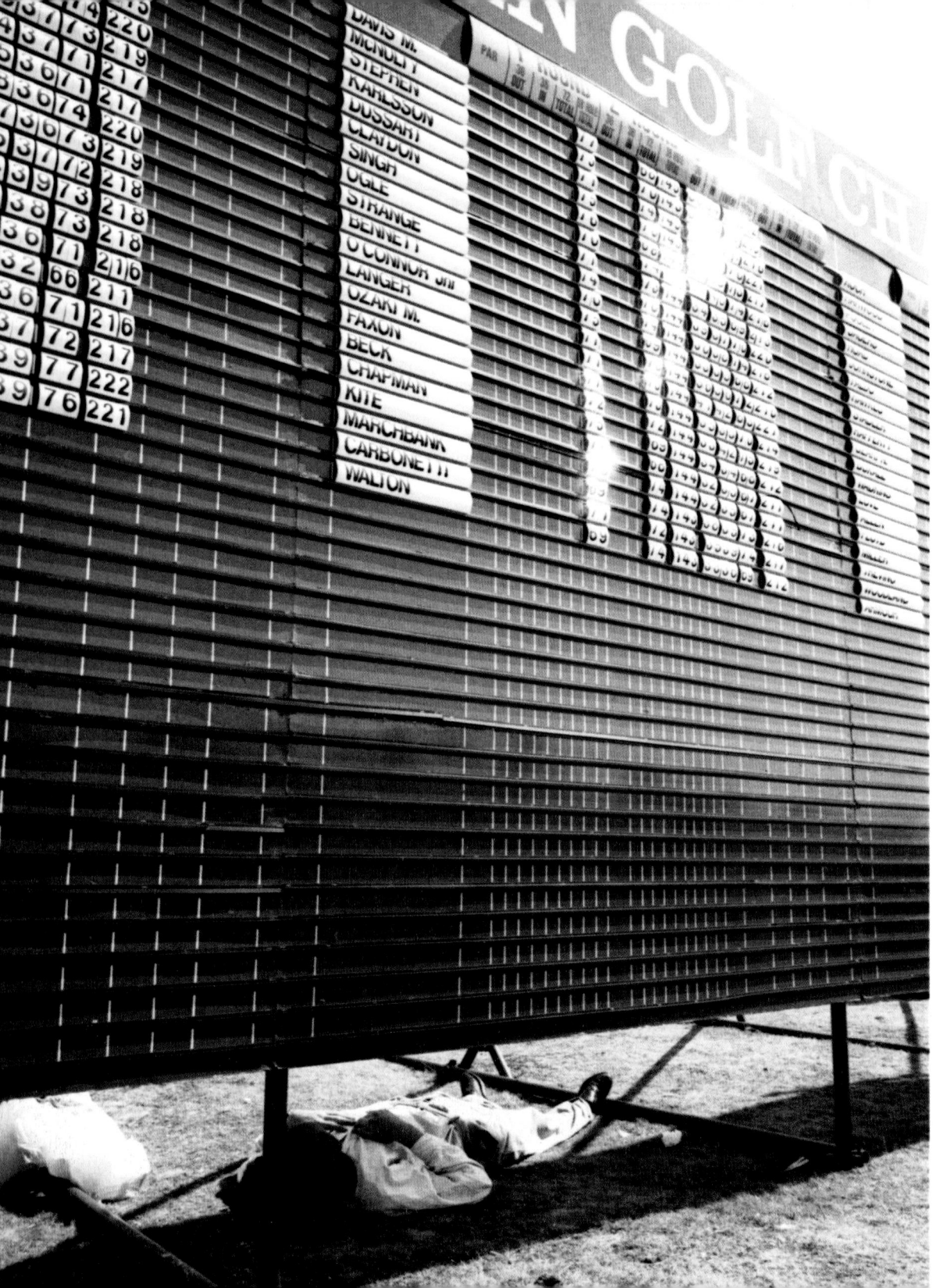

■ Rarely, such as at the Troon Open of 1982 (left), the rains stay away, the skies clear, and Scotland catches the sun. The weather swings to the other extreme and it can get really quite hot (or, at least, hot by Scottish standards).

So hot that caddies have to take the chance of a snooze in the shade wherever they can find it.

No names, no pack drill. No strong liquor was consumed in the making of this photograph!

■ Much more common are weather events that cause trouble.

The photo on the right shows Carnoustie in 1968, the day before The Open was due to start.

The press tent had been blown down by overnight gales and required a hurried re-build.

357

SOMETIMES, just sometimes, the weather is just right.

This is the tented village at the Turnberry Open of 1977.

Not too windy, not too hot, and not a wrath-of-the-gods hailstorm . . . just perfect.

Clear, blue skies on a summer's day, with time to relax and enjoy it all.

And you think to yourself: what a truly wonderful game golf is, and what a magical place Scotland is to watch it or play it.

There's no golf like Scottish golf.

In The Black & White Era
series of sports nostalgia books
By Steve Finan

Thousands of photos of stadiums, football, rugby, and now golf that haven't been seen for decades – and in many cases have never been seen at all. These photos were taken for newspapers and magazines but never used.
There is no other collection of images of sport from past years that can rival this.
These books make up a unique library. The series will continue to be added to.

All titles in the **In The Black & White Era** series are available at **www.dcthomsonshop.co.uk**